1980s

Ten Years of Popular Hits Arranged for **EASY PIANO**

Arranged by Dan Coates

DECADE *by* **DECADE**

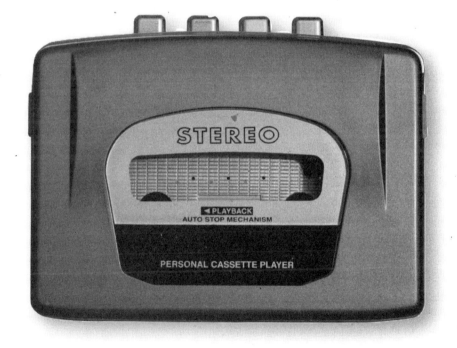

Contents

AFTER ALL
(LOVE THEME FROM *CHANCES ARE*)

Pop icon, Cher, and former lead singer of the rock band Chicago, Peter Cetera, released the duet "After All" in 1989. It was the love theme on the soundtrack to *Chances Are*, a romantic comedy starring Cybill Shepherd, Robert Downey, Jr., Ryan O'Neal, and Mary Stuart Masterson. It was also released on Cher's 20th studio album, *Heart of Stone*, which also included her big hit single "If I Could Turn Back Time" (on page 81).

Words and Music by
Dean Pitchford and Tom Snow
Arranged by Dan Coates

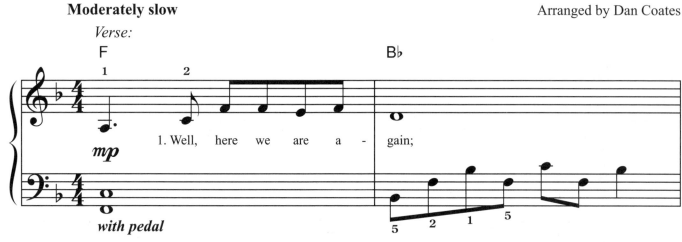

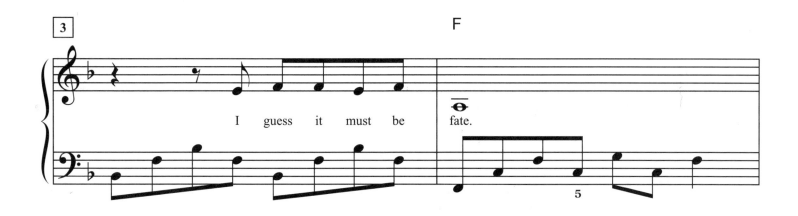

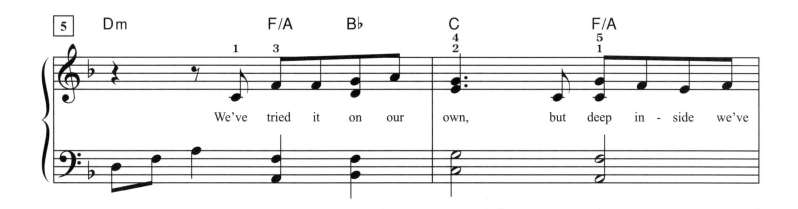

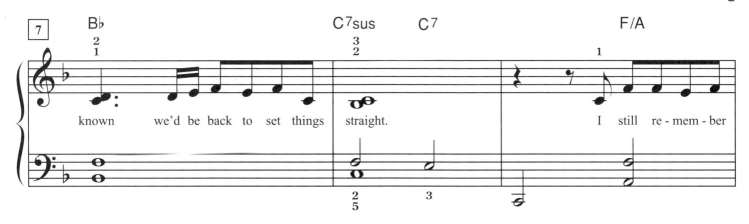

known we'd be back to set things straight. I still re-mem-ber

when your kiss was so brand new. Ev-'ry

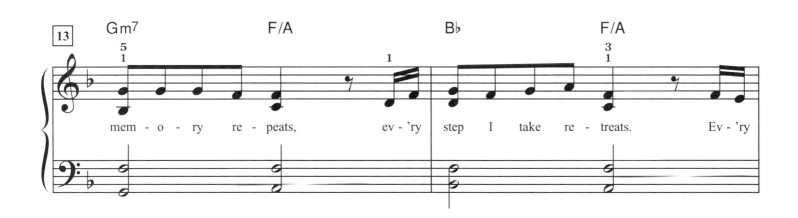

mem-o-ry re-peats, ev-'ry step I take re-treats. Ev-'ry

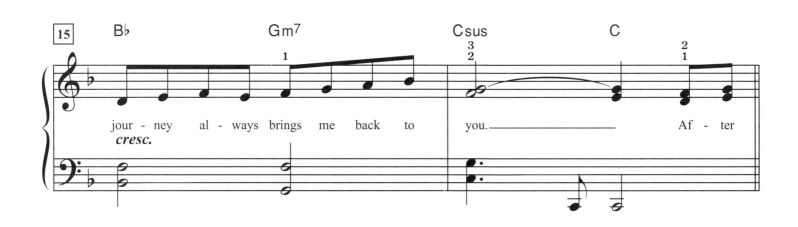

jour-ney al-ways brings me back to you._____ Af-ter

cresc.

%. *Chorus:*

all the stops and starts, we keep com-in' back to these two hearts, two

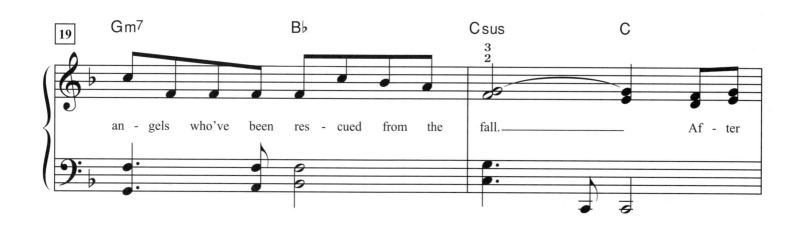

an - gels who've been res - cued from the fall._____ Af - ter

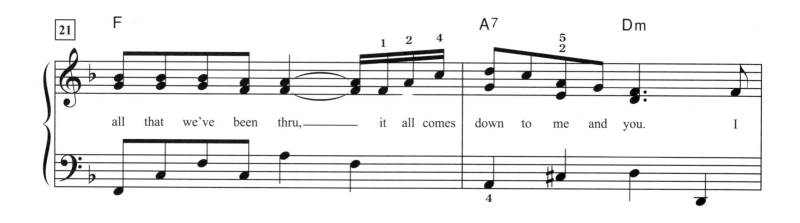

all that we've been thru,_____ it all comes down to me and you. I

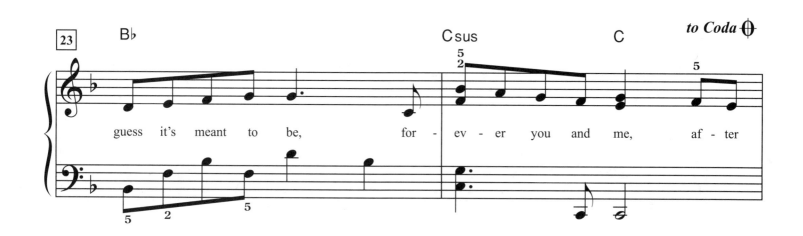

to Coda ⊕

guess it's meant to be, for - ev - er you and me, af - ter

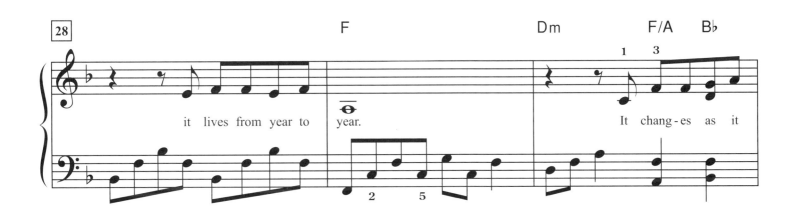

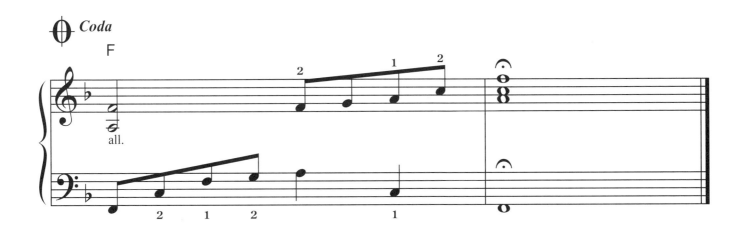

ALWAYS

In 1987 R & B group, Atlantic Starr, topped the Billboard Hot 100 and Billboard R & B charts with "Always." The song was their biggest hit single and was from their album *All in the Name of Love*. Atlantic Starr was also known for their popular hit "Secret Lovers" from their album *As the Band Turns*.

Words and Music by
Jonathan Lewis, Wayne Lewis and David Lewis
Arranged by Dan Coates

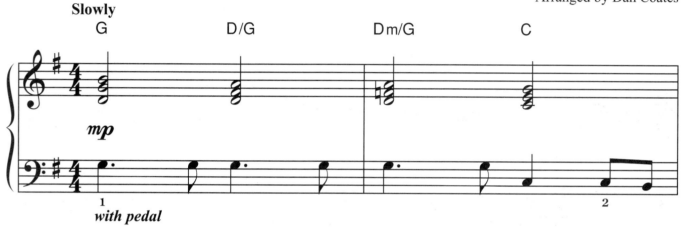

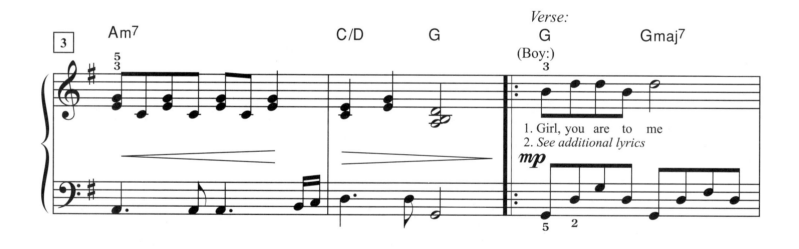

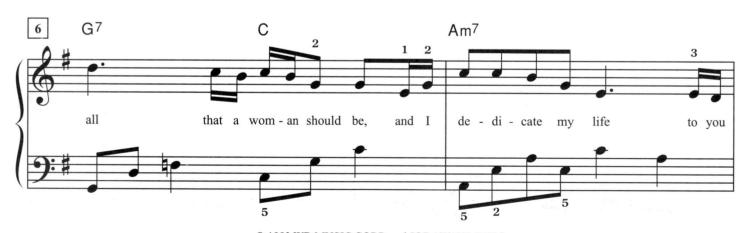

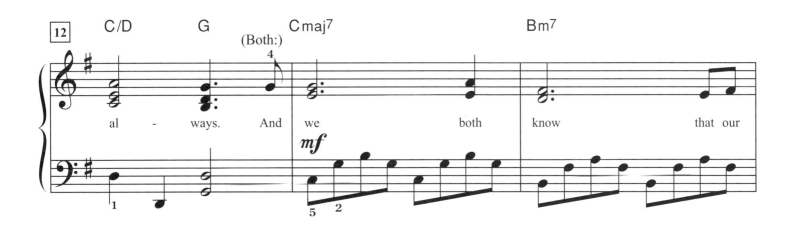

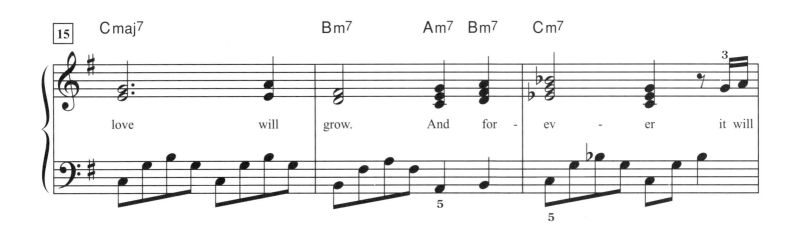

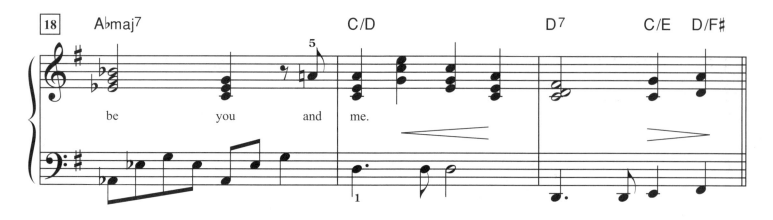

Chorus:

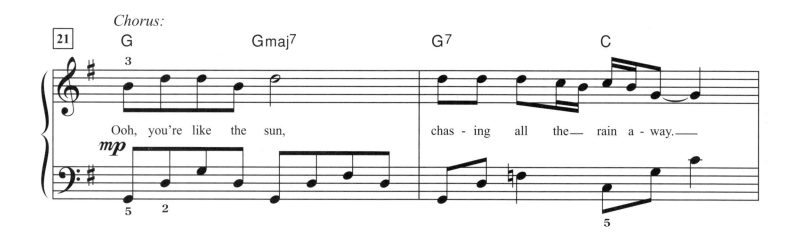

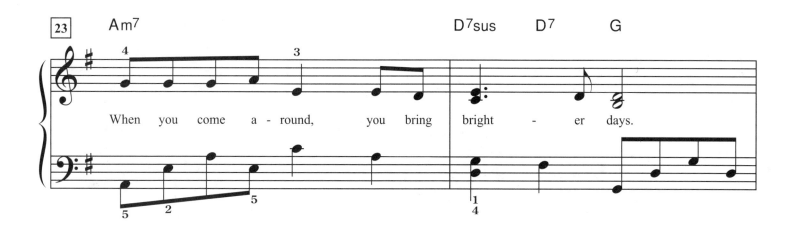

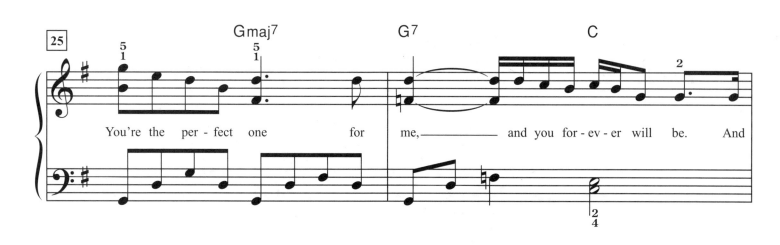

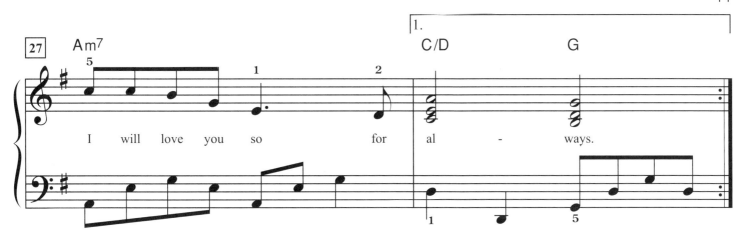

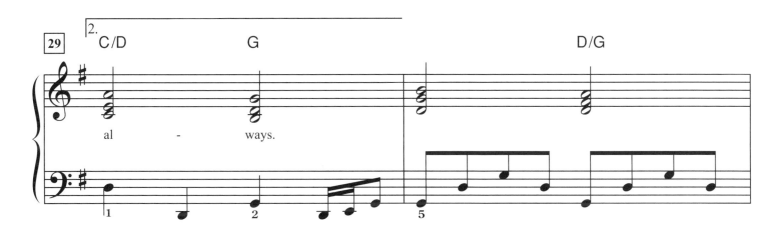

Verse 2:
(Boy:)
Come with me, my sweet;
Let's go make a family.
And they will bring us joy for always.

(Girl:)
Oh, boy, I love you so;
I can't find enough ways to let you know.
But you can be sure I'm yours for always.

(Both:)
And we both know that our love will grow.
And forever it will be you and me.
(To Chorus:)

AT THIS MOMENT

Billy Vera formed The Beaters, a southern California band based on the rock and roll bands of the '50s, with bass player friend Chuck Fiore in 1979. The band played live at the Troubadour in West Hollywood, CA, in the early '80s. In 1985 a producer from the hit sitcom *Family Ties*, attended one of their shows and decided to use their song "At This Moment" in one of the show's episodes. It became extremely popular, peaking at #1 and staying on the charts for 15 weeks.

Words and Music by Billy Vera
Arranged by Dan Coates

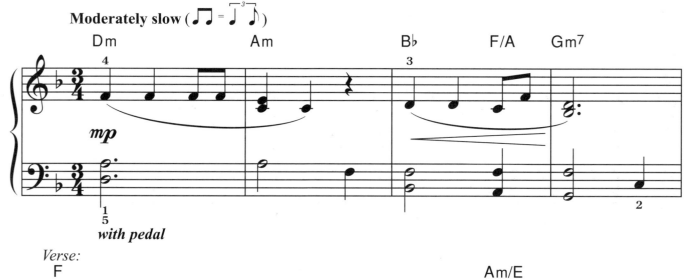

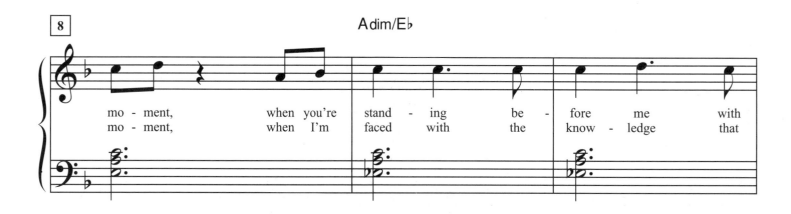

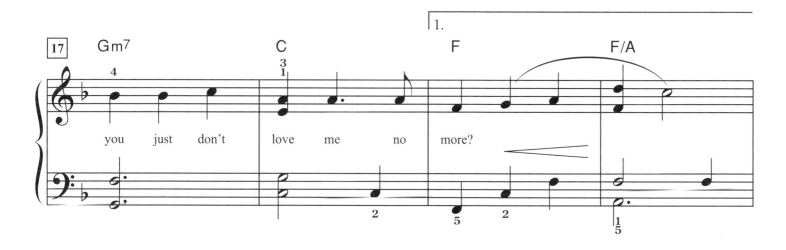

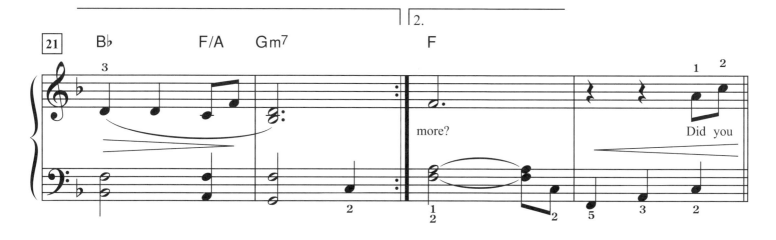

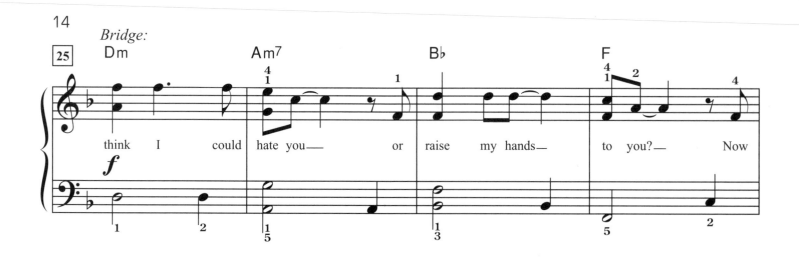

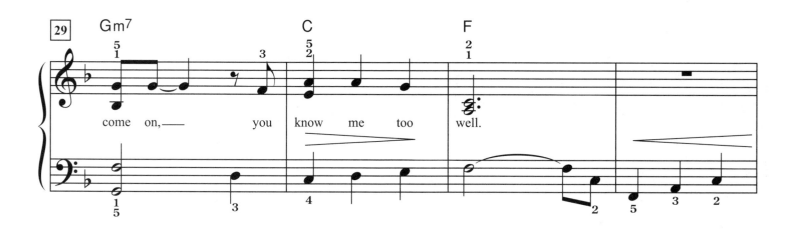

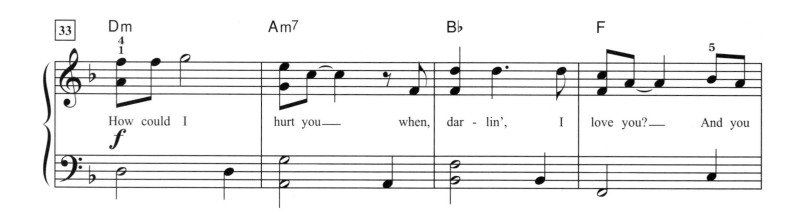

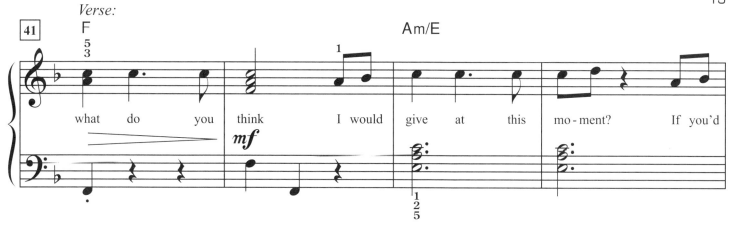

Verse:

41

what do you think I would give at this mo-ment? If you'd

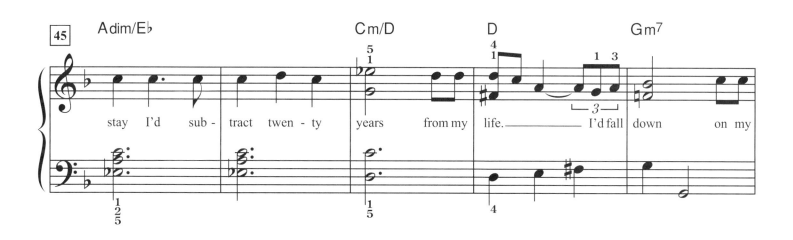

45

stay I'd sub-tract twen-ty years from my life._____ I'd fall down on my

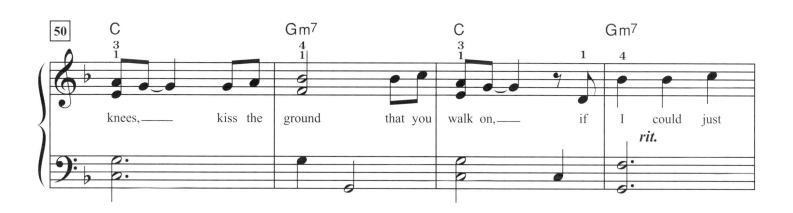

50

knees,_____ kiss the ground that you walk on,_____ if I could just

rit.

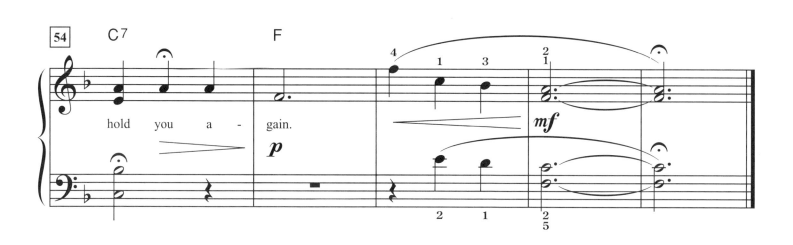

54

hold you a-gain.

BAD

In his 1988 autobiography *Moonwalk*, Michael Jackson wrote: ""Bad" is a song about the street. It's about this kid from a bad neighborhood who gets to go away to a private school. He comes back to the old neighborhood when he's on a break from school, and the kids from the neighborhood start giving him trouble. He sings, 'I'm bad, you're bad, who's bad, who's the best?' He's saying when you're strong and good, then you're bad." "Bad" is from Jackson's 1987 album of the same name which set a record as the only album to produce five #1 singles.

Written and Composed by Michael Jackson
Arranged by Dan Coates

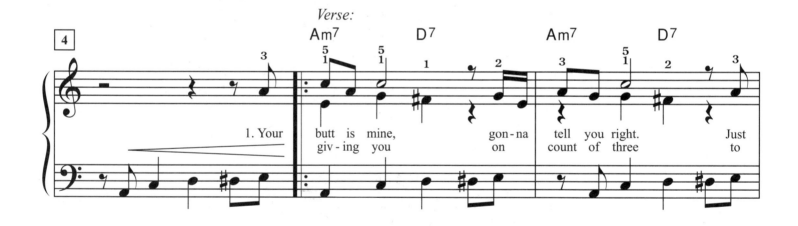

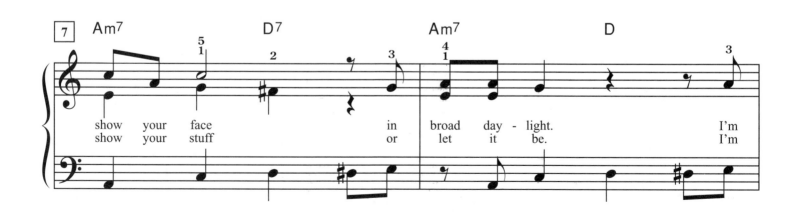

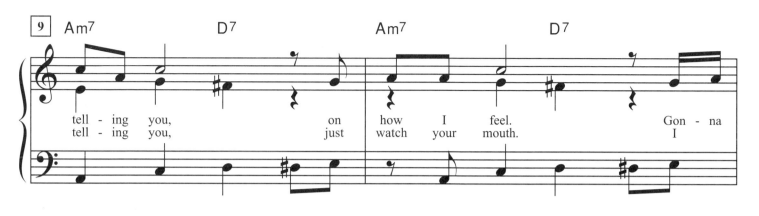

tell - ing you, on how I feel. Gon - na
tell - ing you, just watch your mouth. I

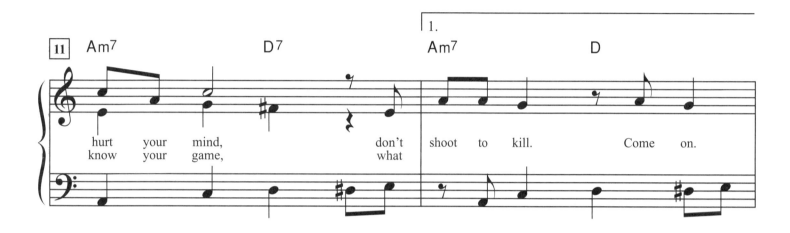

hurt your mind, don't shoot to kill. Come on.
know your game, what

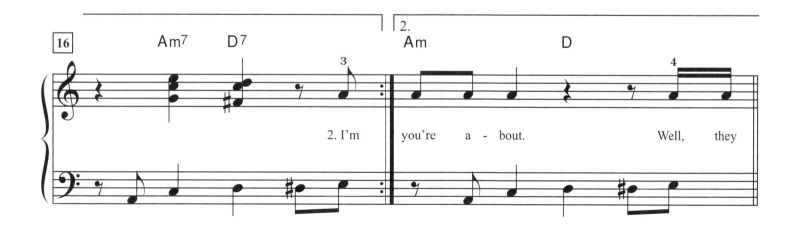

2. I'm you're a - bout. Well, they

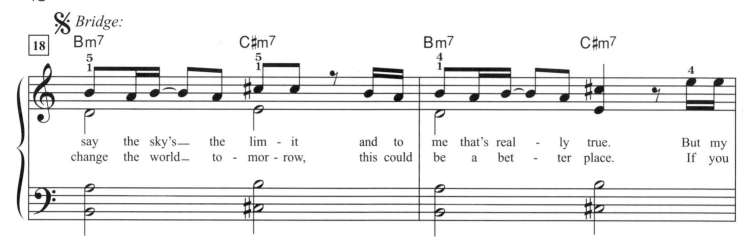

Bridge:
18
Bm7 C♯m7 Bm7 C♯m7
say the sky's the lim - it and to me that's real - ly true. But my
change the world to - mor - row, this could be a bet - ter place. If you
20
Bm7 C♯m7 E7(♯9)
friend, you have seen noth - in'. Just wait 'til I get through
don't like what I'm say - in', then won't you slap my face
be - cause I'm
cresc.
Chorus:
22
Am C/D Am7 C/D Am C/D
bad, I'm bad, come on. You know I'm bad, I'm bad, you
f
25
Am7 C/D Am C/D Am7 D7
to Coda
know it. You know I'm bad, I'm bad, you know it, you know. And the

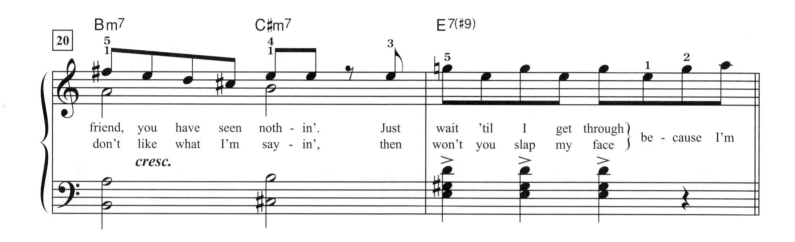

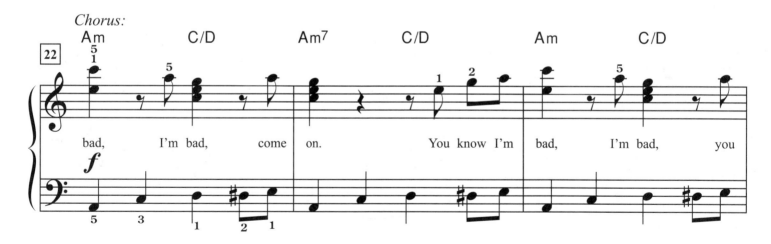

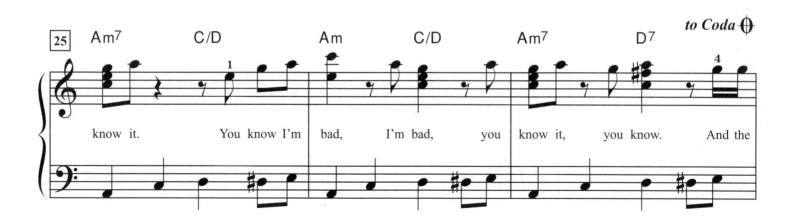

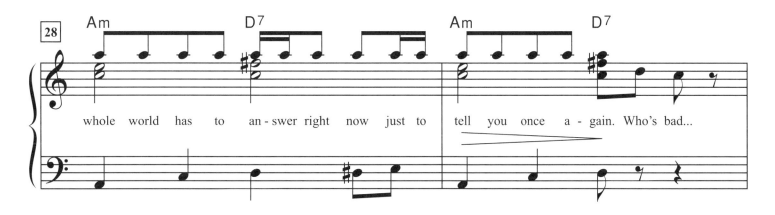

Am   D7   Am   D7

whole world has to an-swer right now just to tell you once a-gain. Who's bad...

N.C.

mp

Verse:

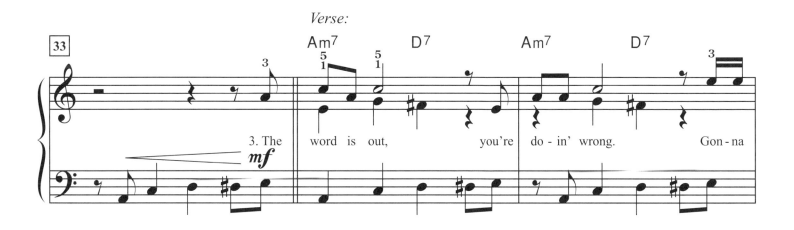

Am7   D7   Am7   D7

3. The word is out, you're do-in' wrong. Gon-na

mf

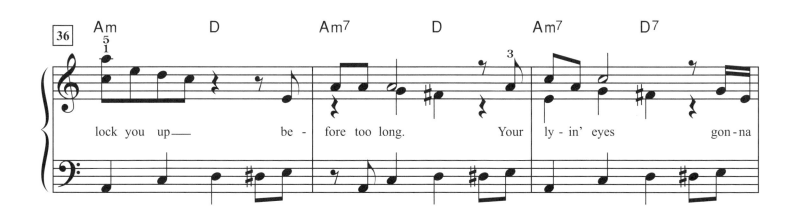

Am   D   Am7   D   Am7   D7

lock you up—— be-fore too long. Your ly-in' eyes gon-na

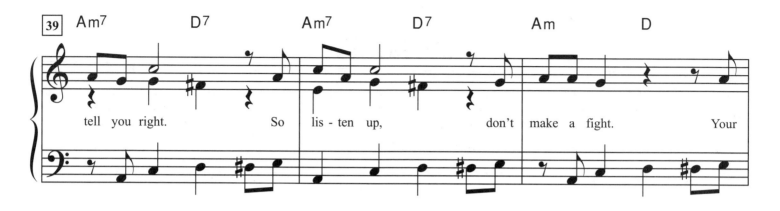

39 Am7   D7   Am7   D7   Am   D

tell you right.   So lis - ten up,   don't make a fight.   Your

42 Am7   D7   Am7   D7

talk is cheap,   you're not a man.   You're

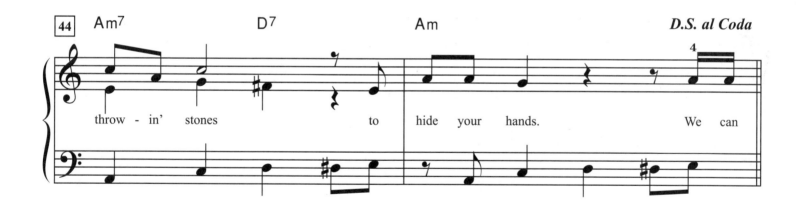

44 Am7   D7   Am   *D.S. al Coda*

4

throw - in' stones   to hide your hands.   We can

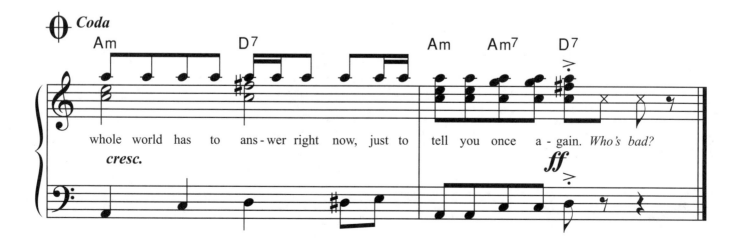

Coda

Am   D7   Am   Am7   D7

whole world has to ans - wer right now, just to   tell you once a - gain. *Who's bad?*

cresc.   **ff**

BEAT IT

"Beat It" is the third hit single from Michael Jackson's album *Thriller* (1982), an album which yielded an unprecedented seven top 10 singles. *Thriller* is the best-selling album of all time and the only album to be the best-selling album for two years in a row. Jackson garnered two Grammy Awards for "Beat It," and it is one of the great crossover hits appealing not only to R & B fans but also to rock fans with Van Halen's special guest guitar solo.

Written and Composed by Michael Jackson
Arranged by Dan Coates

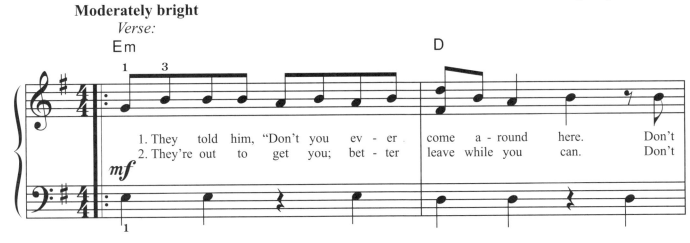

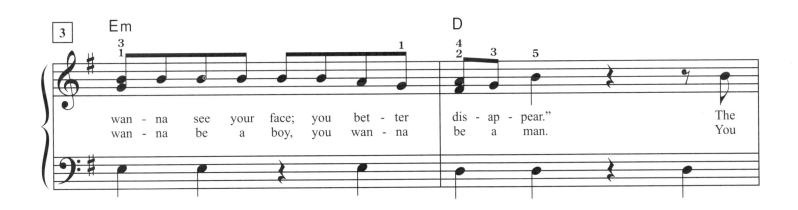

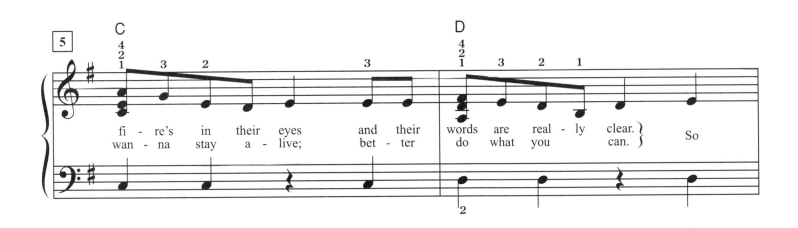

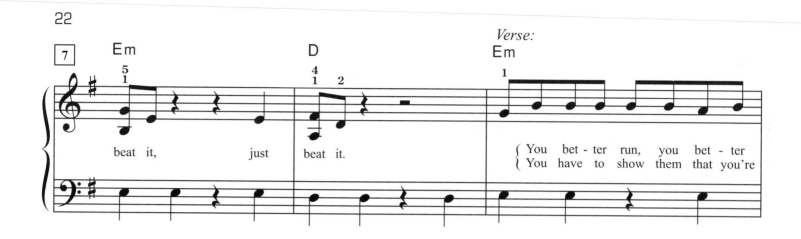

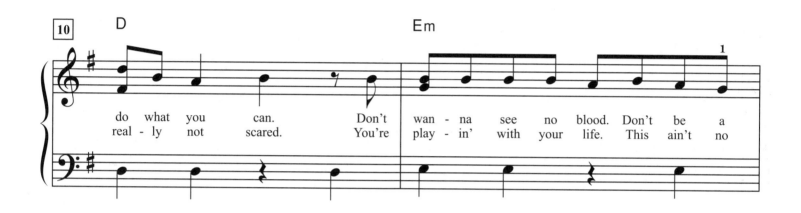

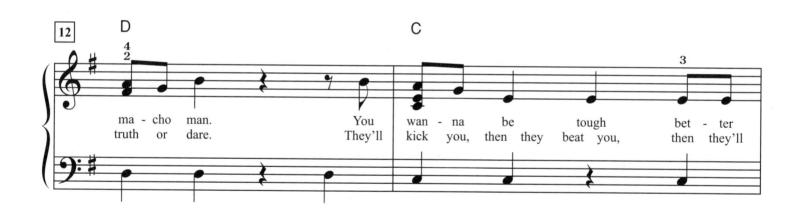

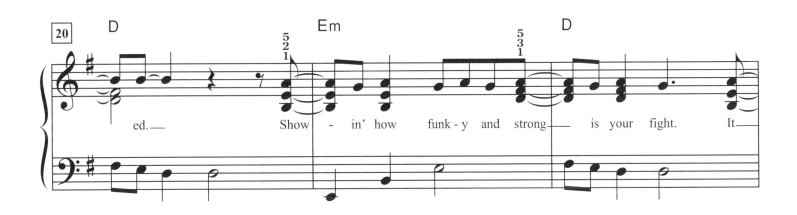

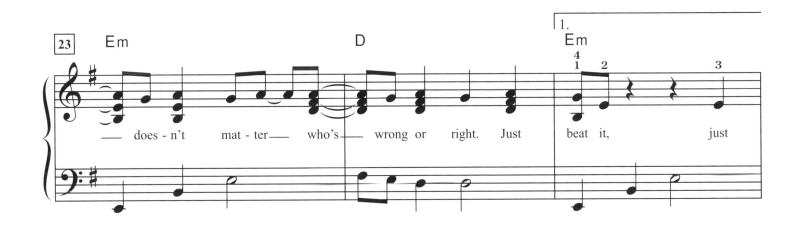

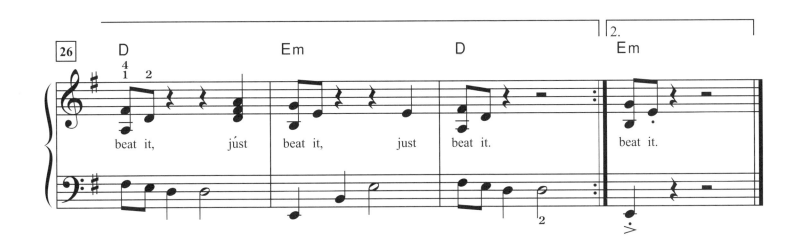

BILLIE JEAN

"Billie Jean" is Michael Jackson's best-selling single. It is from his album *Thriller* (1982). On March 25, 1983, Jackson performed the song for *Motown 25: Yesterday, Today, Forever*, a television special commemorating Motown's 25th anniversary; Jackson performed the song and his signature dance move, the Moonwalk. The music video to "Billie Jean" revolutionized MTV and the music video as a medium; it was the first video to feature an African-American artist and the first video to feature a dance sequence performance by the lead singer.

Written and Composed by Michael Jackson
Arranged by Dan Coates

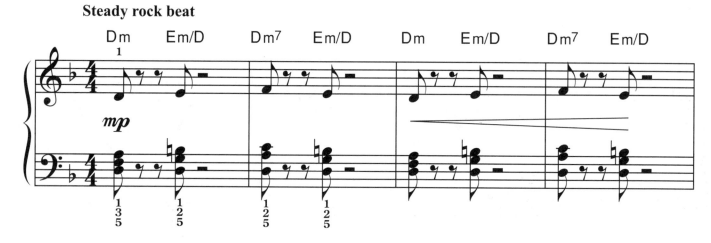

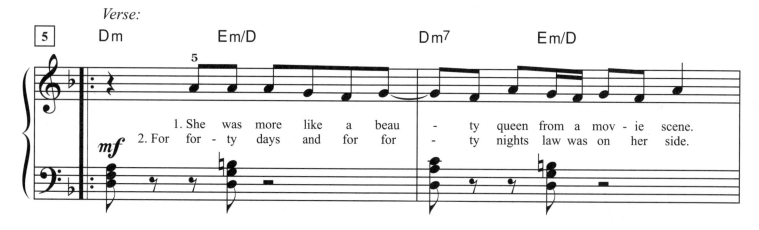

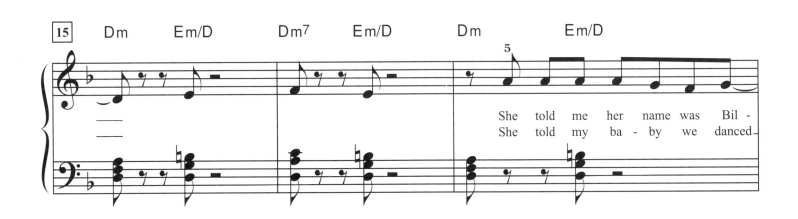

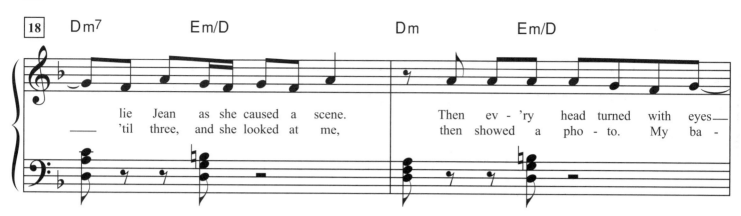

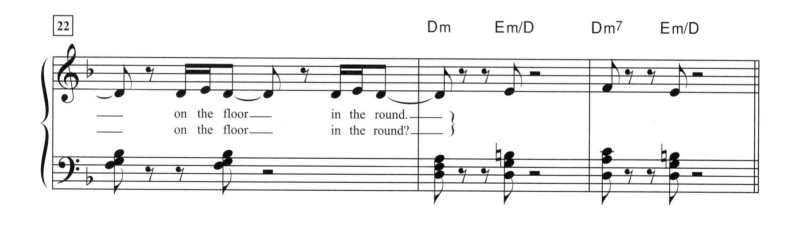

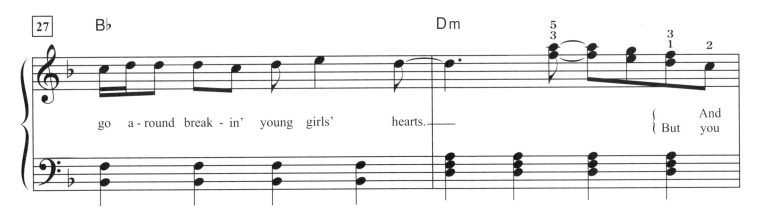

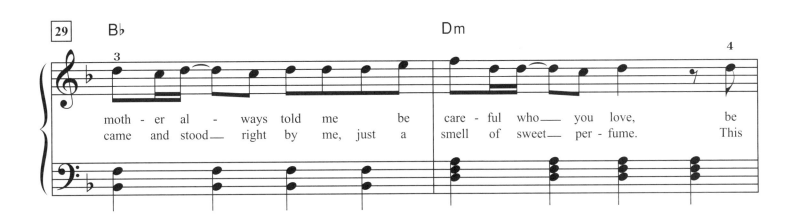

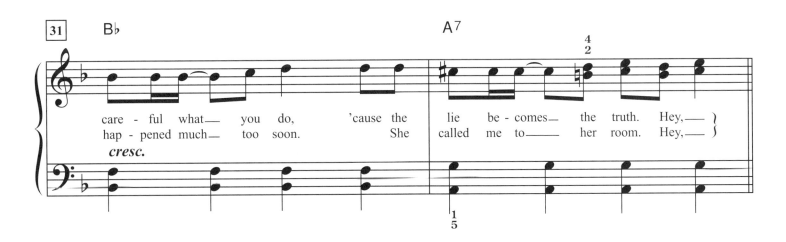

Chorus:

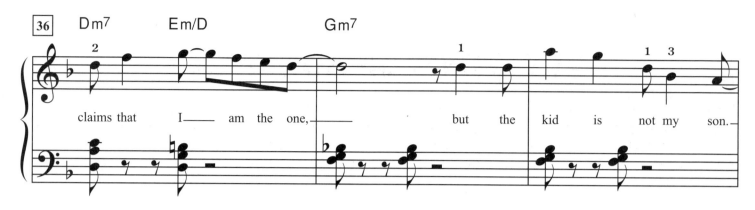

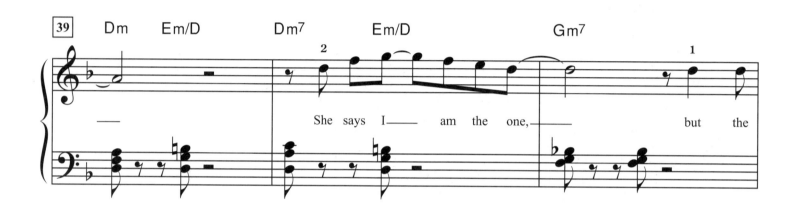

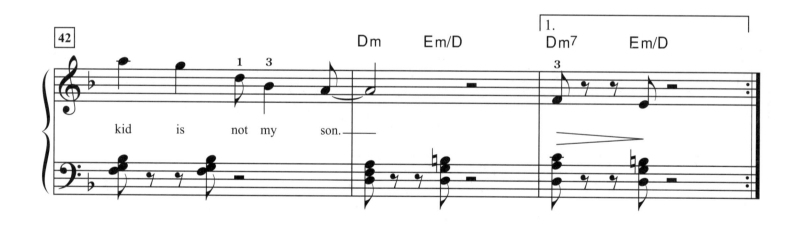

THE BOYS OF SUMMER

"The Boys of Summer" is the lead track and first single from Don Henley's album *Building the Perfect Beast* (1984). For this song about passing from youth into middle-age, Henley won a Grammy Award for Best Male Rock Vocal Performance. The song is quintessentially '80s with synthesizers and drum machines in the instrumentation. The music video won the 1985 MTV Video Music Awards for Best Direction, Best Art Direction, Best Cinematography, and Video of the Year.

Words and Music by
Don Henley and Mike Campbell
Arranged by Dan Coates

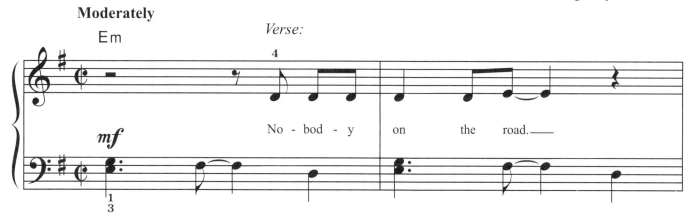

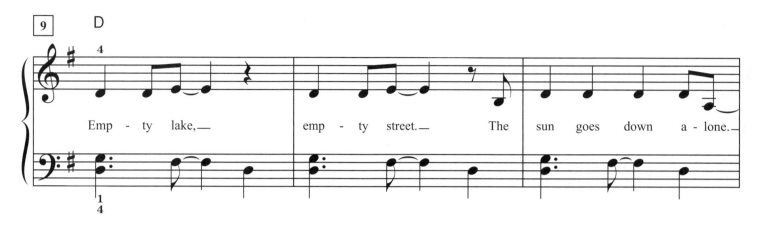

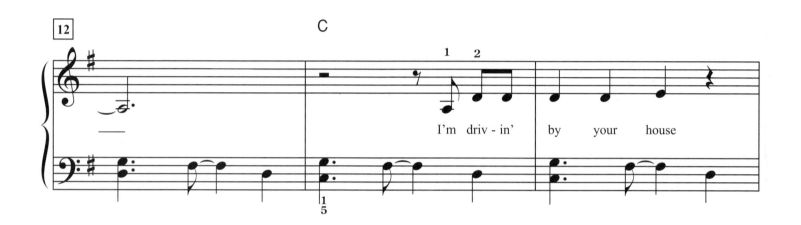

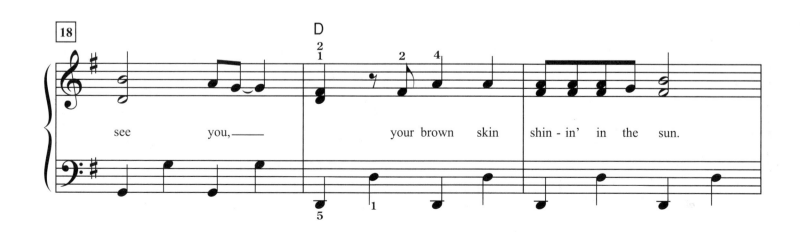

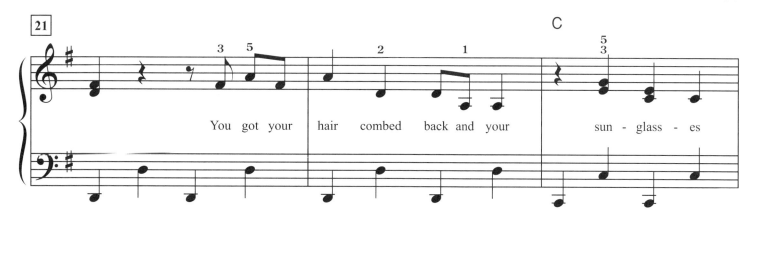

You got your hair combed back and your sun - glass - es

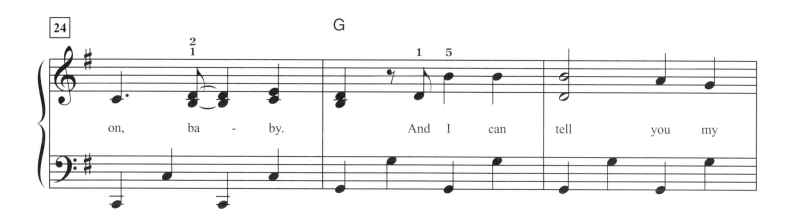

on, ba - by. And I can tell you my

love for you___ will still be strong aft - er___ the

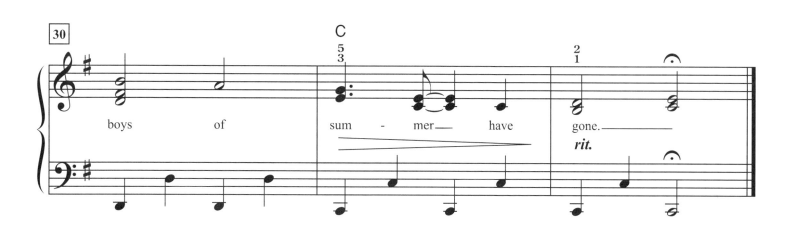

boys of sum - mer___ have gone.___

BROKEN WINGS

"Broken Wings" is a #1 hit single from pop rock band *Mr. Mister*'s second album *Welcome to the Real World* (1985). Lead singer Richard Page and keyboardist Steve George co-wrote the song with Page's cousin John Lang and found inspiration in the book *Broken Wings* by poet Khalil Gibran. The song is notable for utilizing various digital effects including the sound of a crash symbol played in reverse and a digitally delayed electric guitar.

Words and Music by
Richard Page, Steve George and John Lang
Arranged by Dan Coates

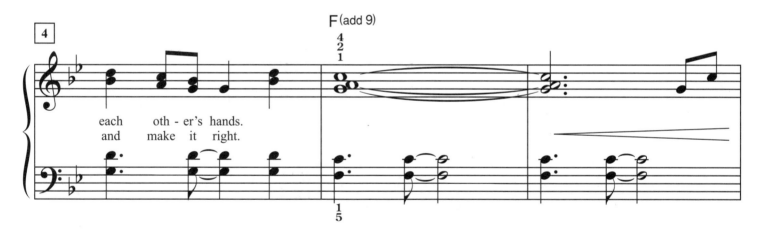

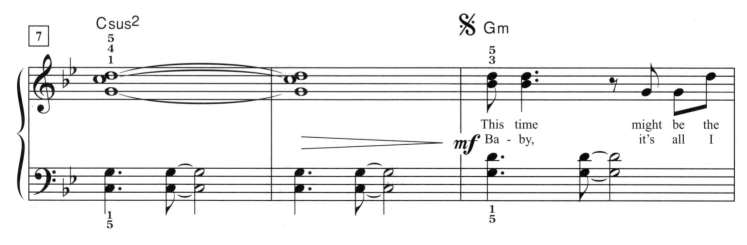

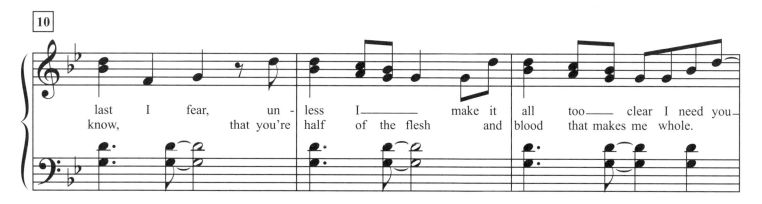

last I fear, un - less I make it all too clear I need you
know, that you're half of the flesh and blood that makes me whole.

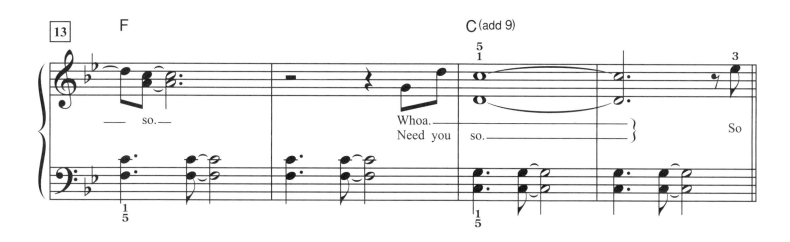

F   C (add 9)

— so.— Whoa.
Need you so.— So

Chorus:

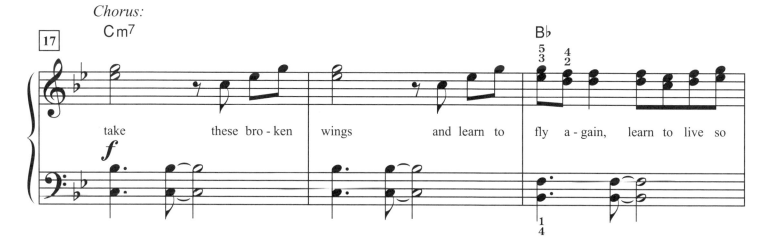

Cm7   B♭

take these bro - ken wings and learn to fly a - gain, learn to live so

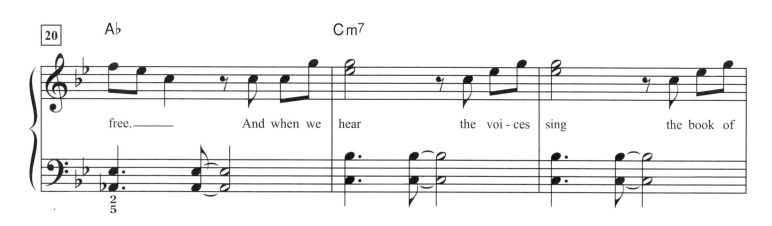

A♭   Cm7

free.— And when we hear the voi - ces sing the book of

34

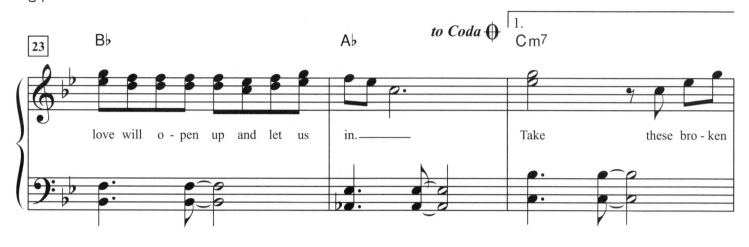

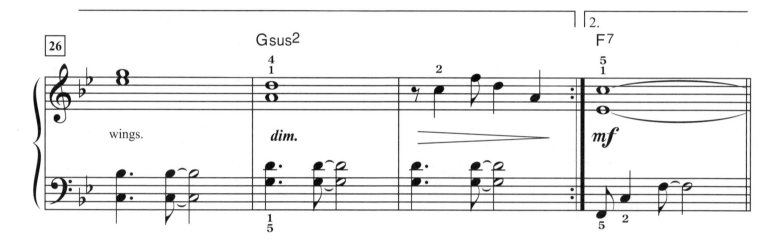

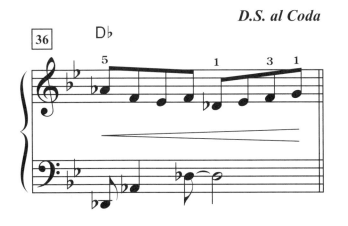
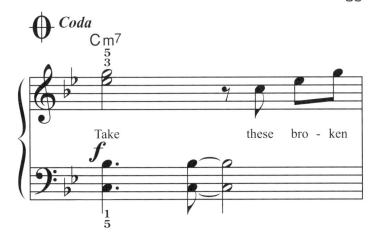
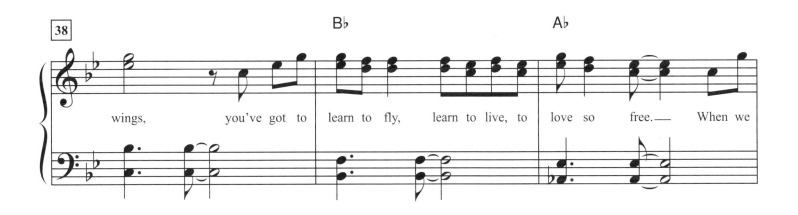
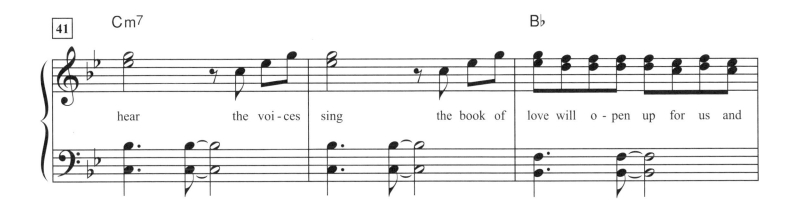
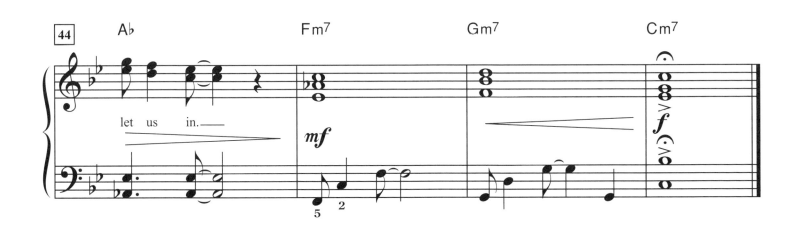

CHERISH

In 1989 "Cherish" became pop icon Madonna's 17th straight top 10 single. It was initially released on her controversial fourth album *Like a Prayer*, an album which incorporated rock, dance, pop, soul, and funk elements. The album included a duet with R & B pop singer Prince as well as references to her mother's death and her divorce from actor Sean Penn.

Words and Music by
Madonna Ciccone and Pat Leonard
Arranged by Dan Coates

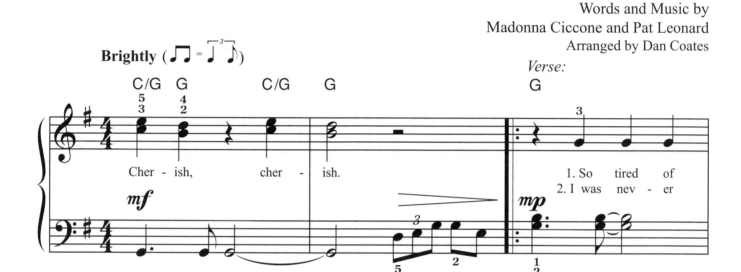

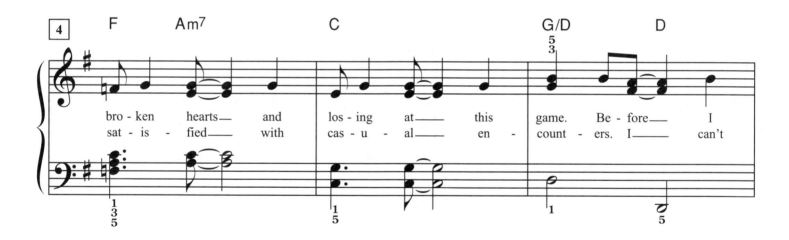

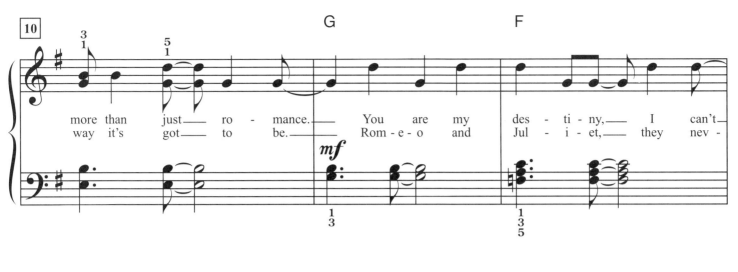

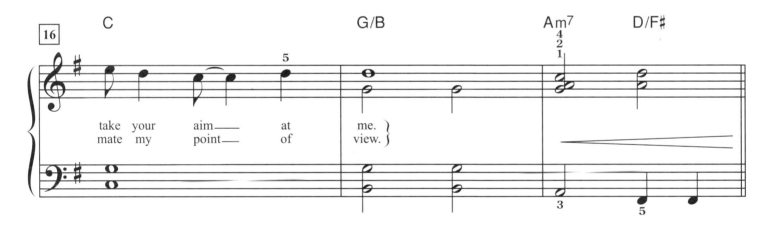

Oh, ba - by, I cher - ish the joy, ___ you keep bring - ing it

in - to my life. ___ I'm al - ways sing - ing it. Cher - ish the strength, ___

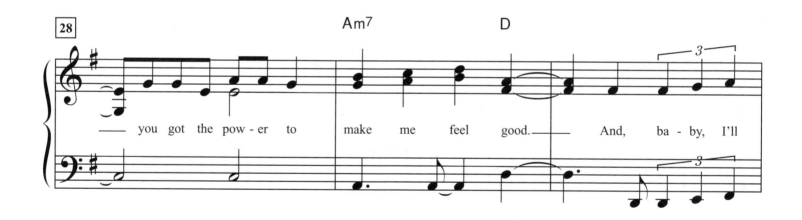

___ you got the pow - er to make me feel good. ___ And, ba - by, I'll

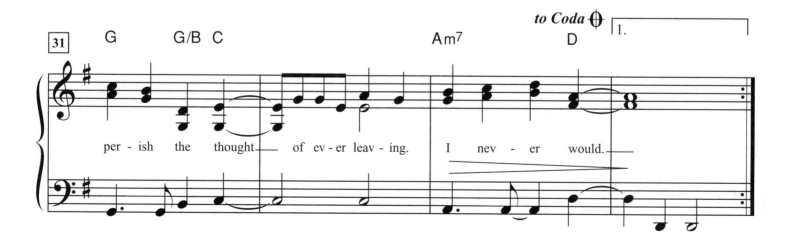

per - ish the thought ___ of ev - er leav - ing. I nev - er would. ___

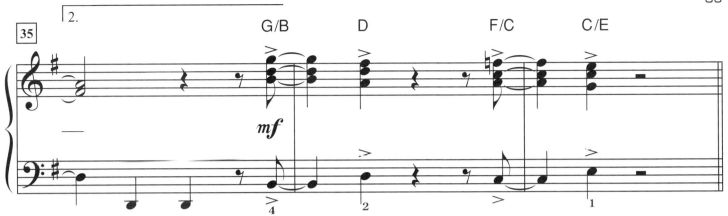
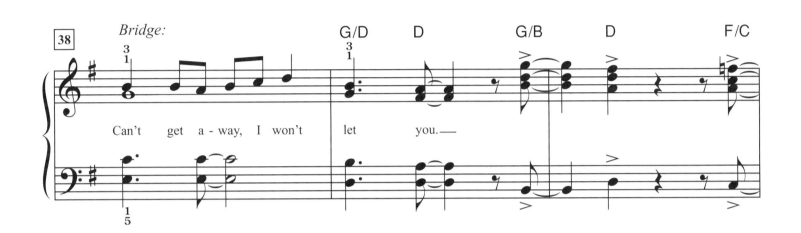

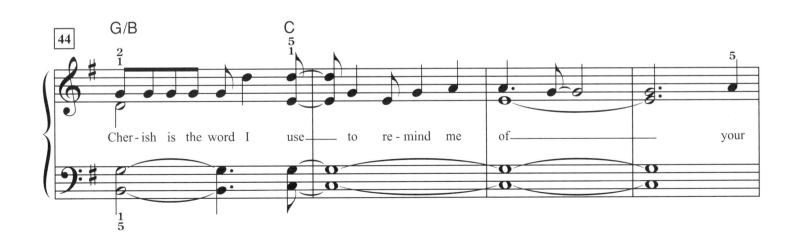

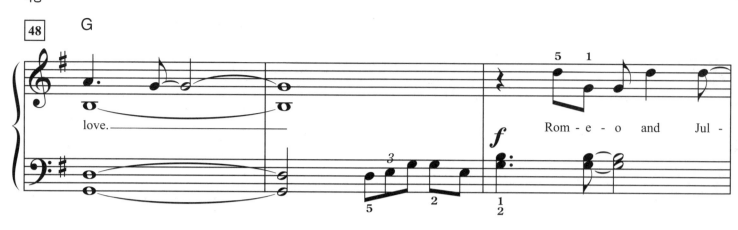

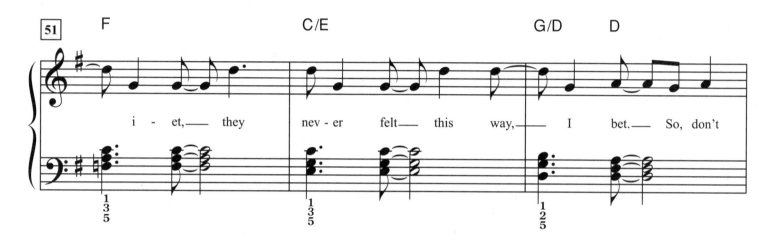

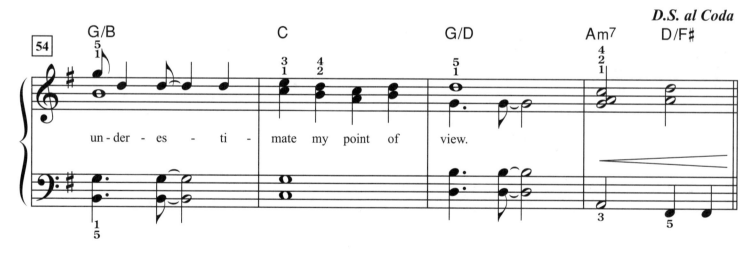

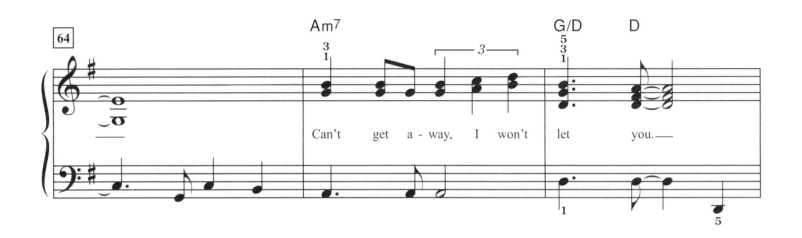

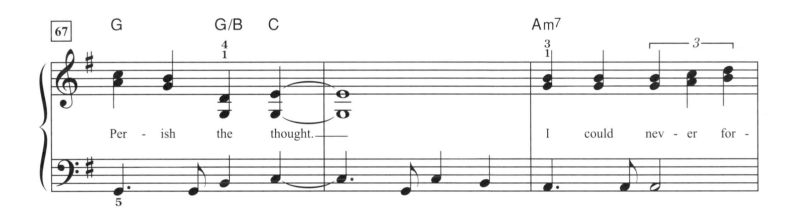

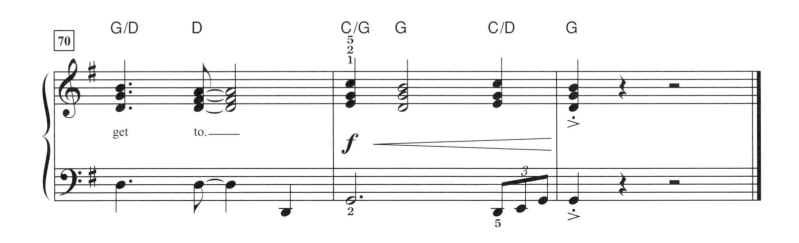

CRAZY FOR YOU

"Crazy for You" was Madonna's second #1 hit in the U.S. It was featured in the 1985 coming-of-age drama *Vision Quest*, starring Matthew Modine and Linda Fiorentino. In the movie, Madonna makes an appearance (her first in a major motion picture) as a singer at a local bar where she performs two songs: "Crazy for You" and "Gambler."

Words and Music by
John Bettis and Jon Lind
Arranged by Dan Coates

Moderately

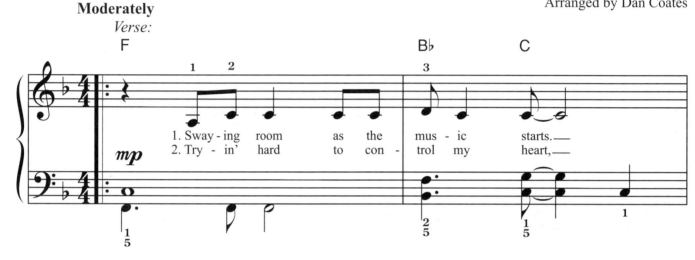

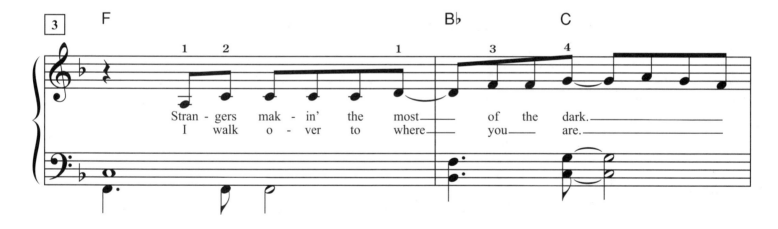

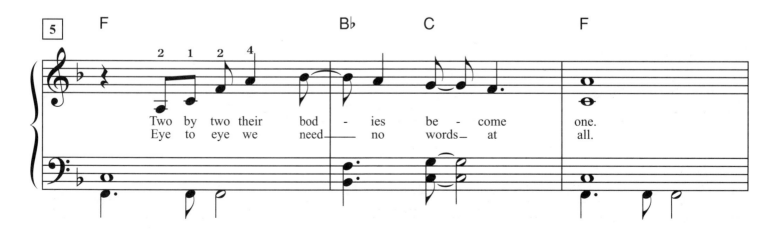

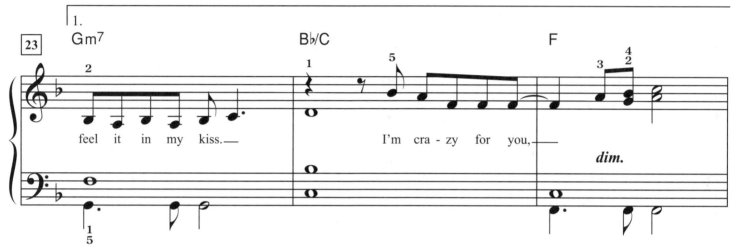

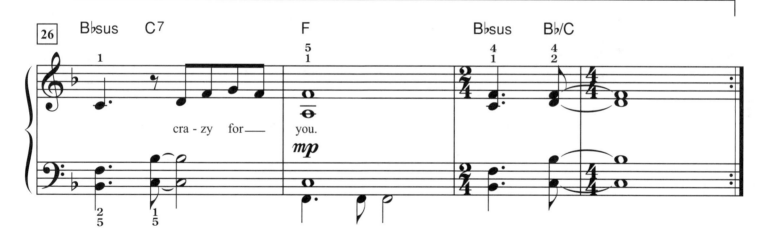

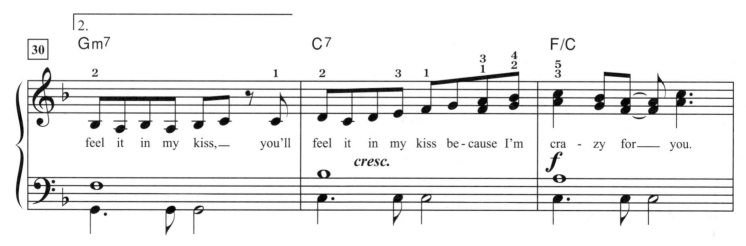

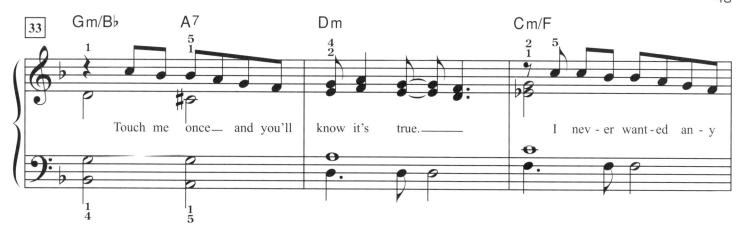

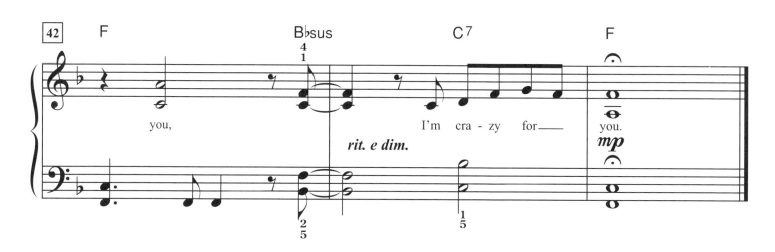

DON'T YOU KNOW WHAT THE NIGHT CAN DO?

Steve Winwood's solo career spans over three decades. He has been a member of the bands The Spencer Davis Group, Traffic, Go, and Blind Faith. His 1988 rock and blue-eyed soul solo album, *Roll with It*, topped the Billboard 200 and won a Grammy Award. "Don't You Know What the Night Can Do?" was one of the hit singles from that album.

Words and Music by
Steve Winwood and Will Jennings
Arranged by Dan Coates

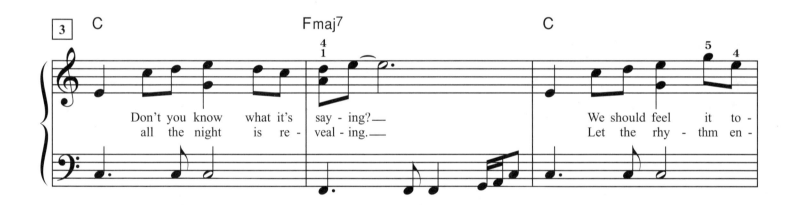

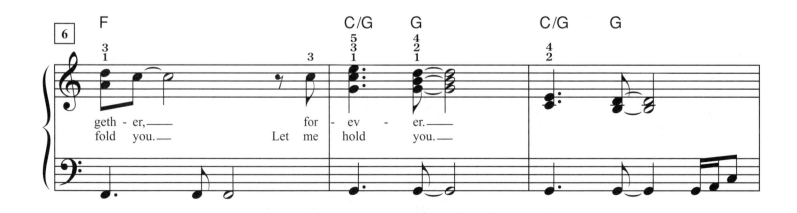

Feel— the beat and just hold on to the sweet mid-night
Now— we turn in - to mu - sic. Now we nev - er will

flow - ing.— Feel the mu - sic in - side— you.—
lose it.— When the rhy - thm and night— ride—

I'll be there, too. Now's the time when our
no heart can hide. There are times that

dreams are fi - n'lly com - ing true. Feels so good, we'rc cry - ing.—
nev - er, ev - er come a - gain. Mem - 'ries there for mak - ing.—

48

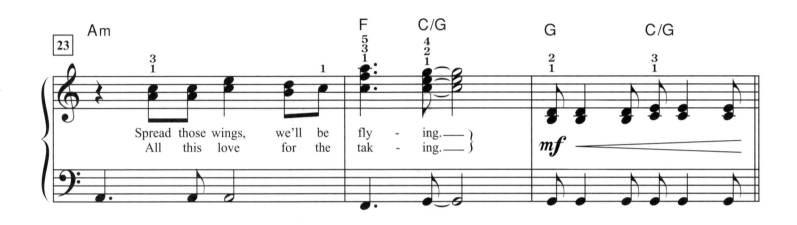

Chorus:

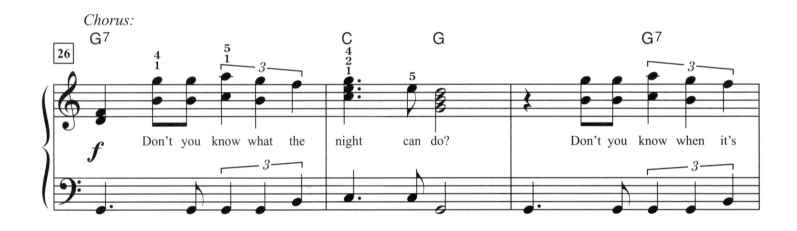

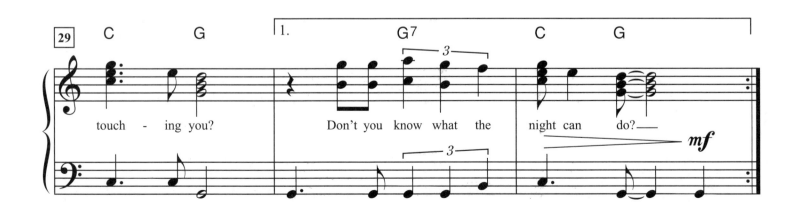

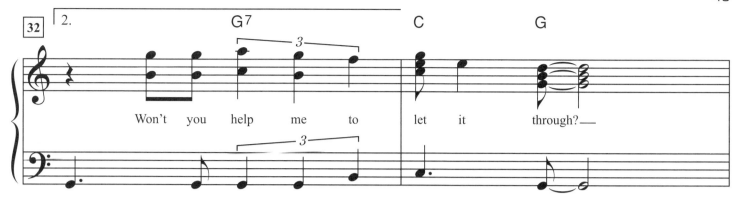

Won't you help me to let it through?—

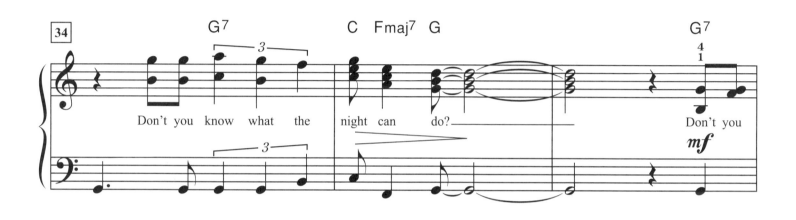

Don't you know what the night can do?—

Don't you

know what the night can do? Know what the night can do? Don't you

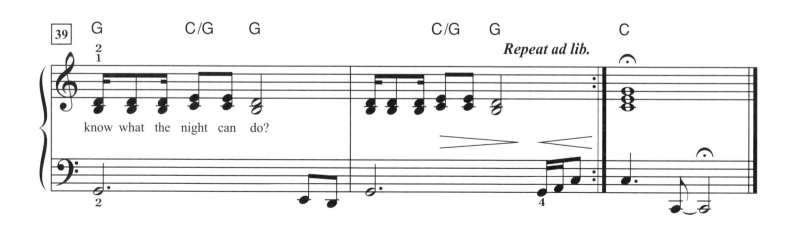

know what the night can do?

Repeat ad lib.

DRIVE

Originally from Boston, the American new wave rock band The Cars emerged in the late '70s and were one of the first bands to merge the sounds of '70s guitar-rock and '80s synthesizer-pop. "Drive" is from their 1984 album *Heartbreak City*. The song gained wide popularity after being featured during *Live Aid*, a 1985 international multi-venue concert aimed at raising funds for famine in Ethiopia.

Words and Music by Ric Ocasek
Arranged by Dan Coates

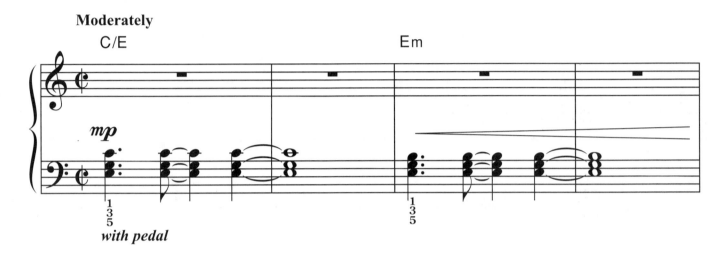

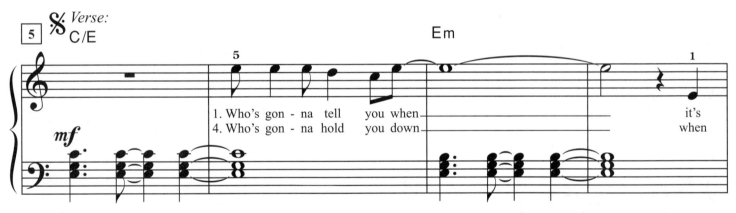

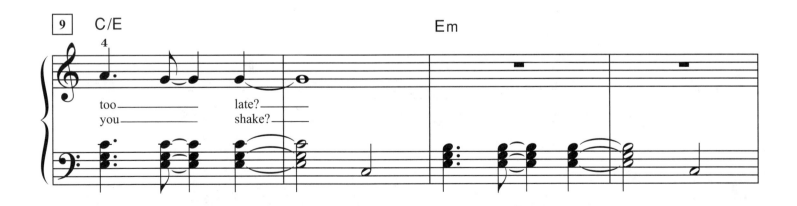

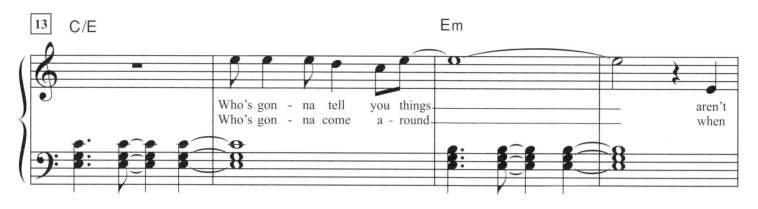

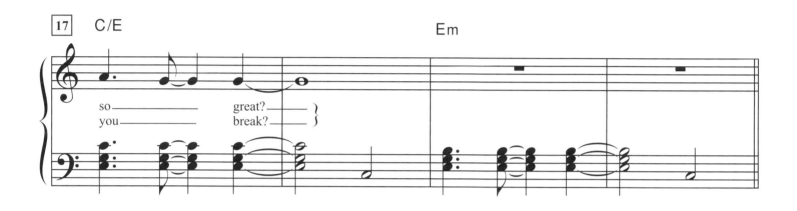

Chorus:

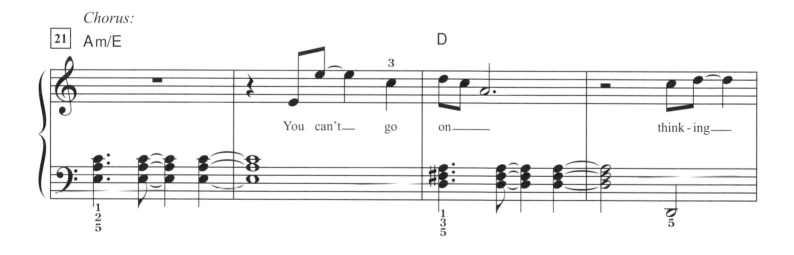

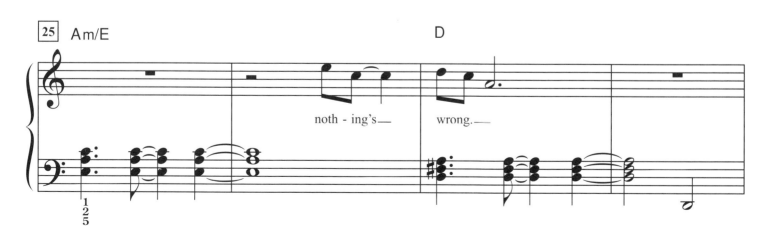

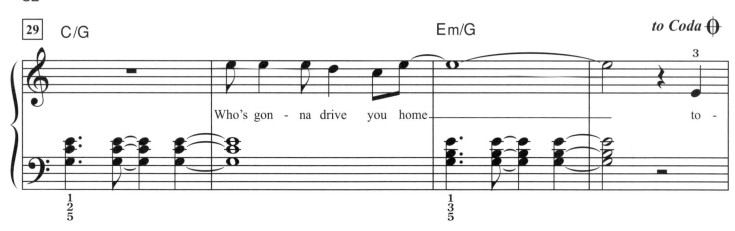

Who's gon - na drive you home_____ to -

night?_____

Verse:

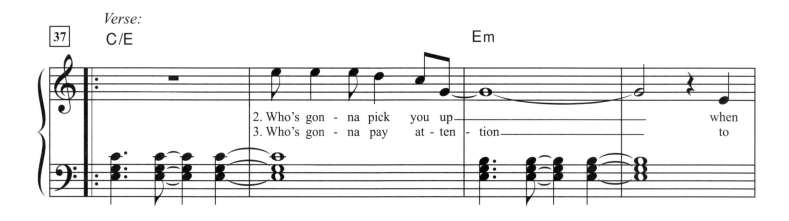

2. Who's gon - na pick you up_____ when to
3. Who's gon - na pay at - ten - tion_____ to

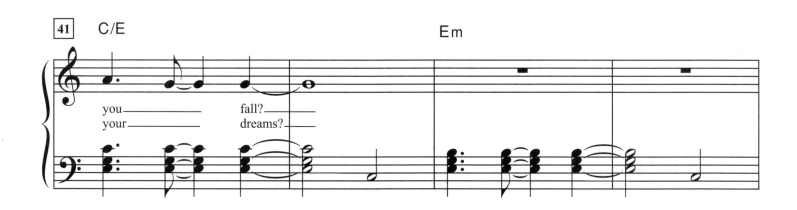

you_____ fall?_____
your_____ dreams?_____

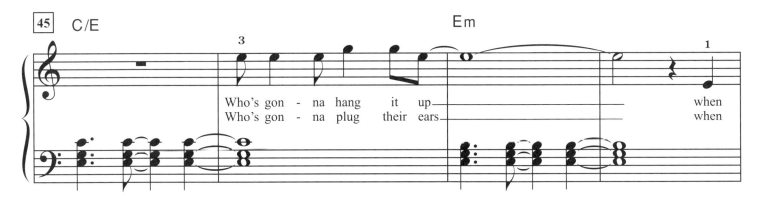

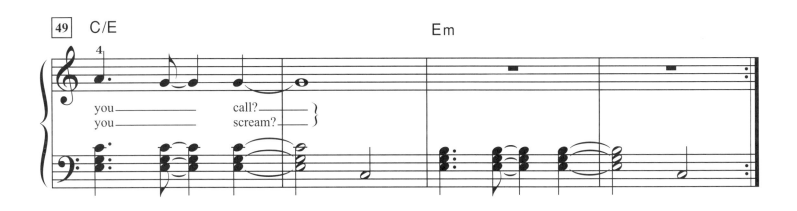

Chorus:

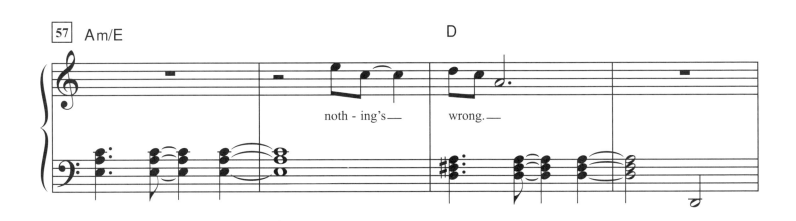

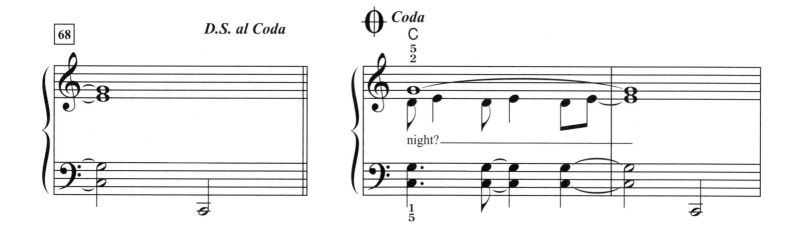

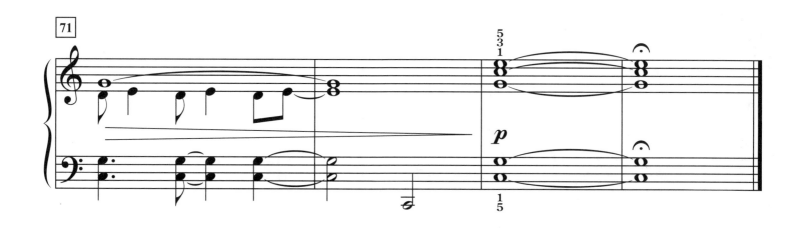

ENDLESS LOVE

Soul singer Diana Ross and pop singer Lionel Richie recorded "Endless Love" in 1981 for the romantic drama of the same name. The movie was directed by Franco Zeffirelli and starred Brooke Shields and Martin Hewitt. The film was a commercial failure, but the song became the biggest-selling single of the year and has become one of the most popular duet ballads of all time. It was covered by Luther Vandross and Mariah Carey in 1994.

Words and Music by Lionel Richie
Arranged by Dan Coates

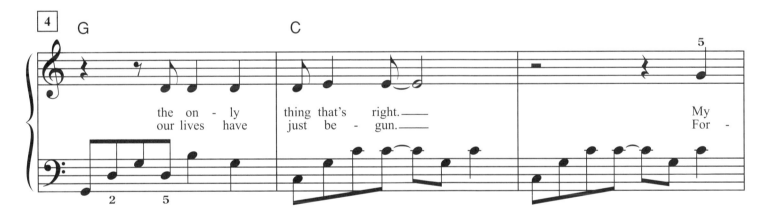

34 G | C G/B | Am Em/G

I'll be that fool for you,————— I'm

37 F | G | C

sure; you—— know I don't mind.

40 B♭/C C | F | G

And yes,——————— you'll be the

43 C | Am Em/G | Fmaj⁷

on - ly—— one.———————— No—— one can de -

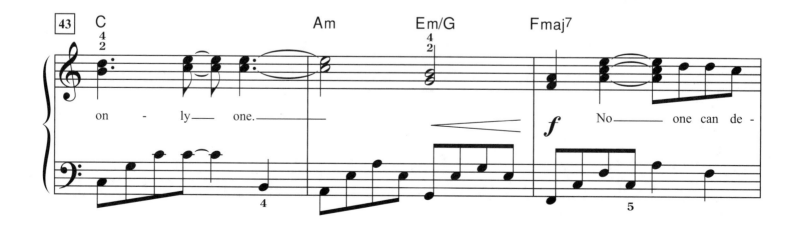

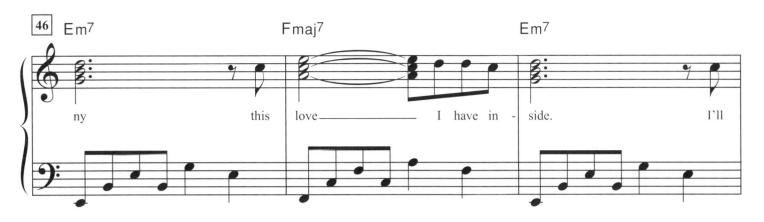

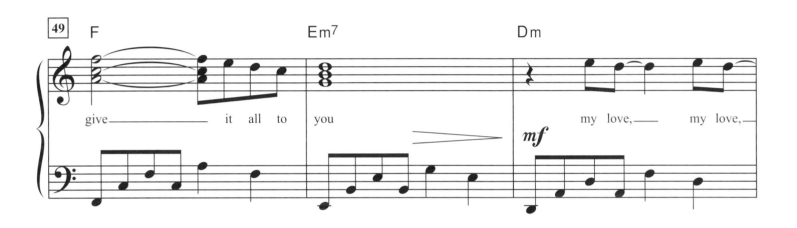

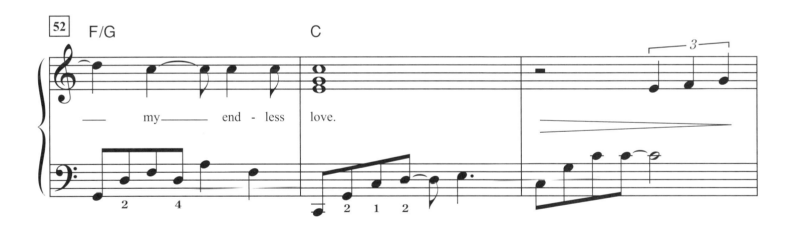

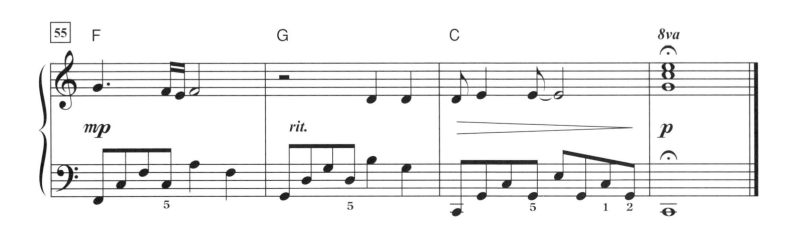

EYE OF THE TIGER

Sylvester Stallone asked the rock band Survivor to write a theme song for *Rocky III* (1982), the third of six movies about a boxer from Philadelphia. "Eye of the Tiger" was the result and became a smash hit, topping the Billboard Hot 100 for six weeks and winning a Grammy Award. The title of the hard rock anthem was based on a line from the movie's script, which had been written by Stallone.

Words and Music by
Frankie Sullivan III and Jim Peterik
Arranged by Dan Coates

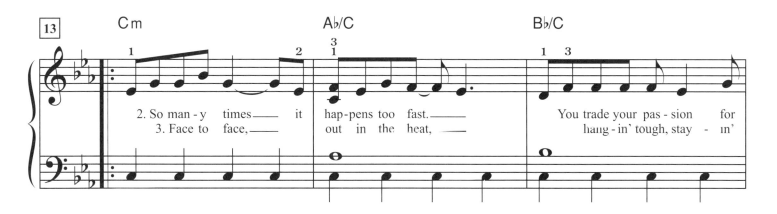

13 Cm   A♭/C   B♭/C

2. So man-y times____ it hap-pens too fast.____ You trade your pas-sion for
3. Face to face,____ out in the heat,____ hang-in' tough, stay-in'

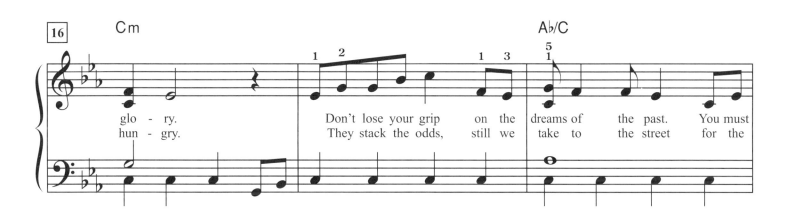

16 Cm   A♭/C

glo - ry. Don't lose your grip on the dreams of the past. You must
hun - gry. They stack the odds, still we take to the street for the

Chorus:

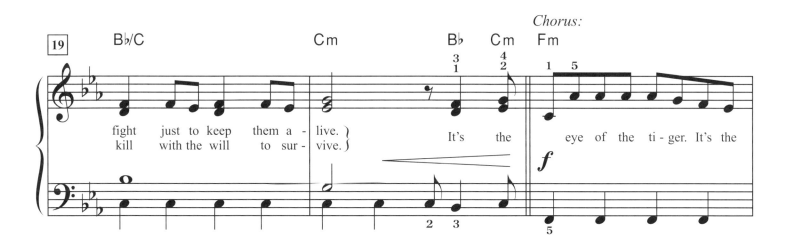

19 B♭/C   Cm   B♭   Cm   Fm

fight just to keep them a - live. It's the eye of the ti-ger. It's the
kill with the will to sur - vive.

f

22 E♭/G   B♭   Cm   Fm   Cm   B♭   Cm

thrill of the fight, ris - in' up to the chal-lenge of our ri - val. And the

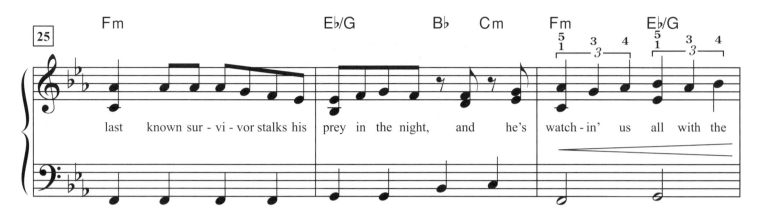

last known sur - vi - vor stalks his prey in the night, and he's watch - in' us all with the

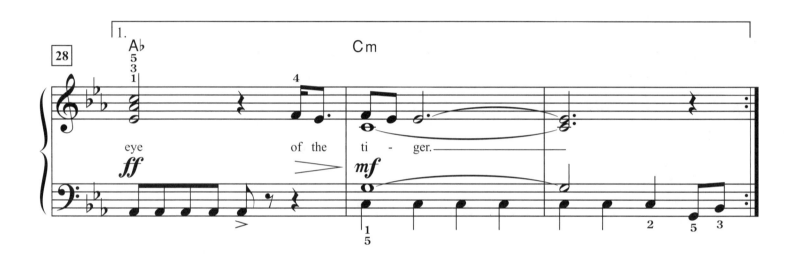

eye of the ti - ger.

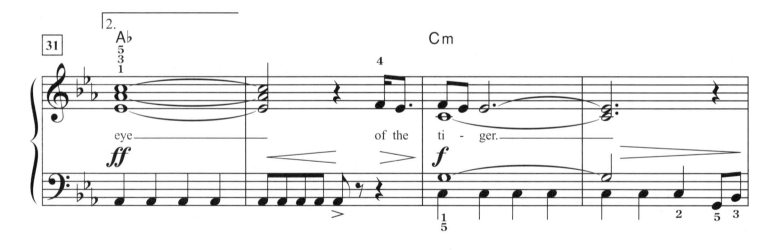

eye of the ti - ger.

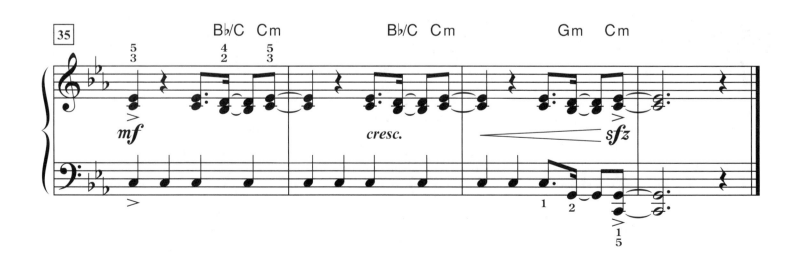

HIGHER LOVE

Steve Winwood released "Higher Love" in 1986. It was the first single from his album *Back in the High Life*, and it was his first #1 hit. It also garnered him two Grammy Awards—Best Male Pop Vocal Performance and Record of the Year. R & B singer Chaka Khan sang backup vocals for the song.

Words and Music by
Steve Winwood and Will Jennings
Arranged by Dan Coates

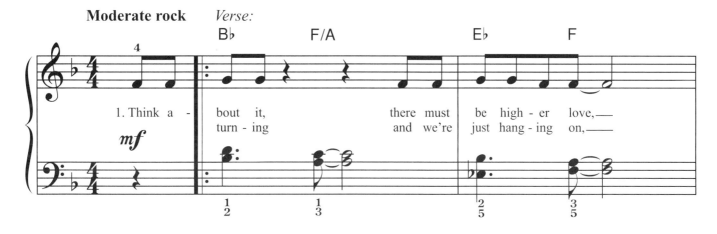

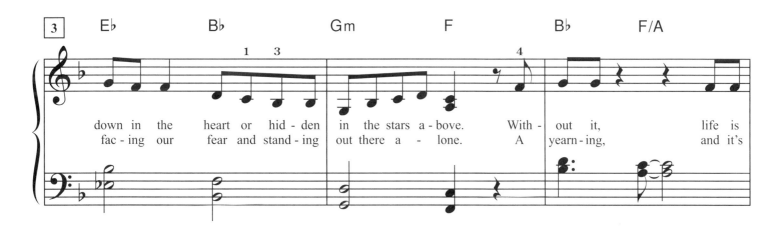

Bridge:

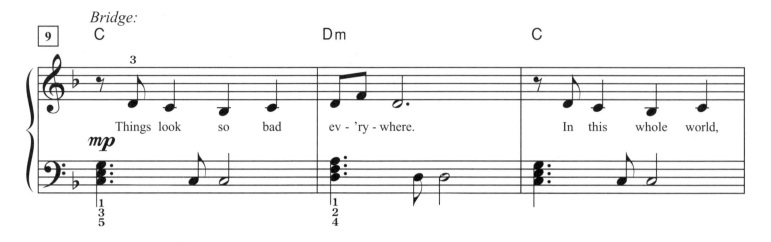

Things look so bad ev - 'ry - where. In this whole world,

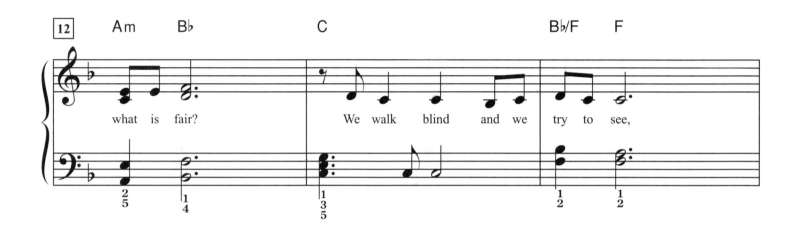

what is fair? We walk blind and we try to see,

Chorus:

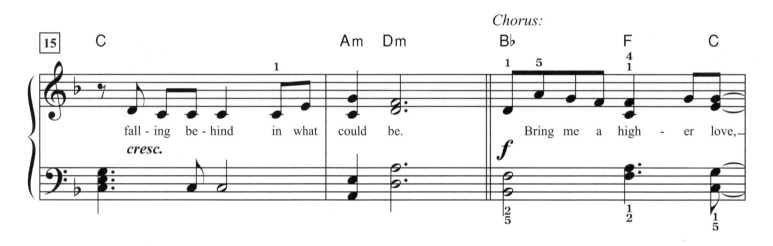

fall - ing be - hind in what could be. Bring me a high - er love,

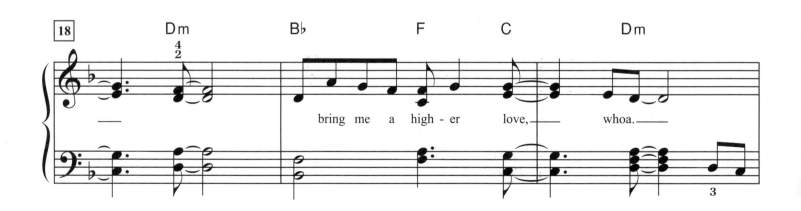

bring me a high - er love, whoa.

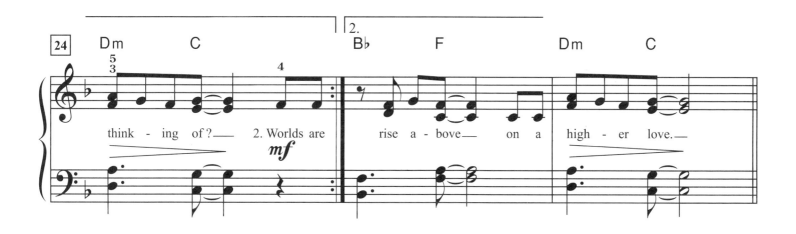

Bridge:

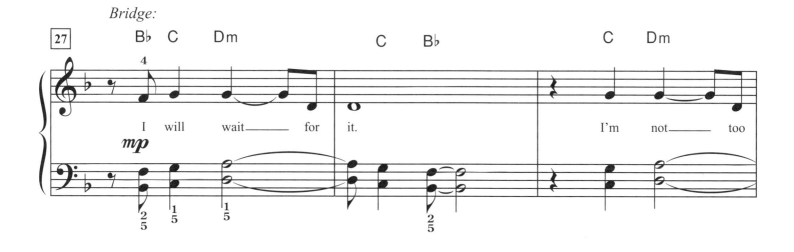

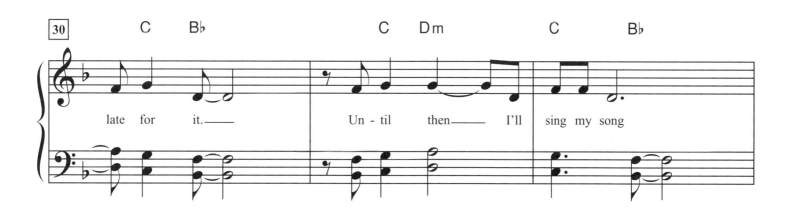

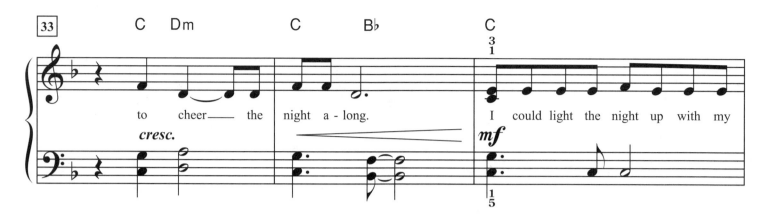

to cheer the night a - long. I could light the night up with my

cresc. *mf*

soul on fire, I could make the sun shine from pure de - sire.

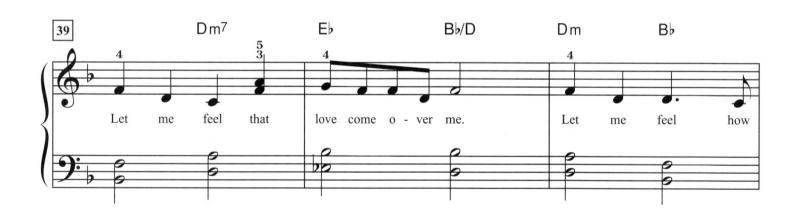

Let me feel that love come o - ver me. Let me feel how

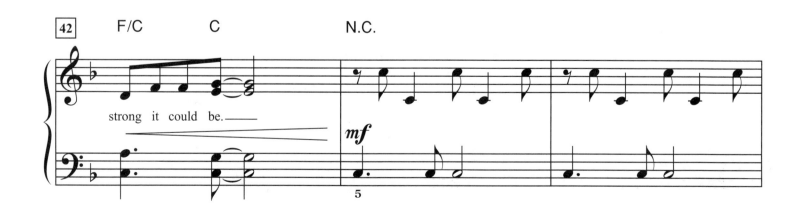

strong it could be. *mf*

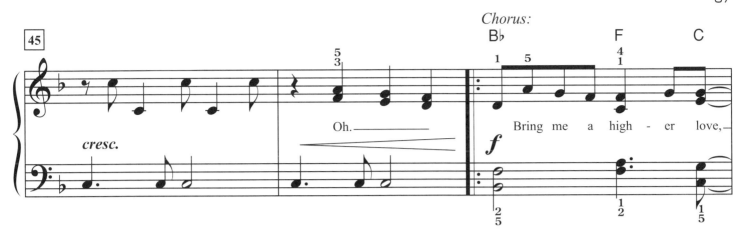

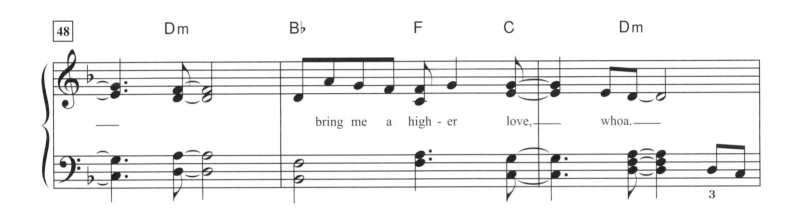

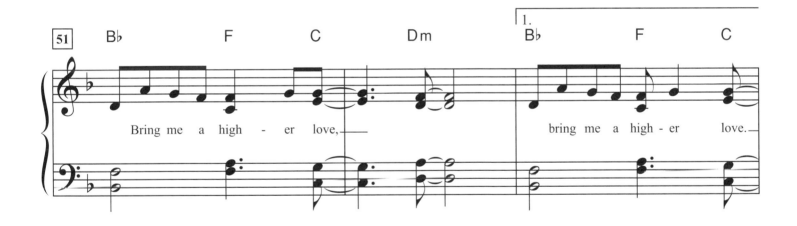

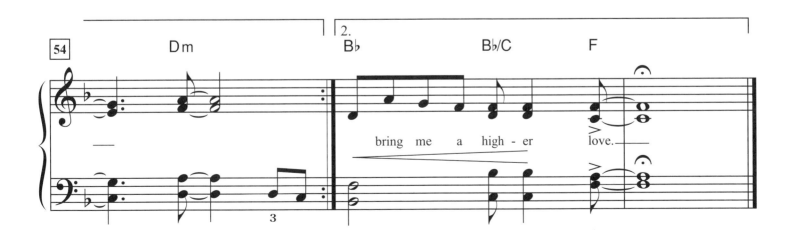

FAME

Fame is a 1980 musical film about students at the New York High School of Performing Arts. The music from the film was critically successful; "Fame" won the Academy Award and Golden Globe Award for Best Original Song, and the score won an Academy Award as well. Irene Cara, who played Coco Hernandez in the film, recorded "Fame" as well as "Out Here on My Own," another single from the soundtrack which was also nominated for an Academy Award.

Music by Michael Gore
Lyrics by Dean Pitchford
Arranged by Dan Coates

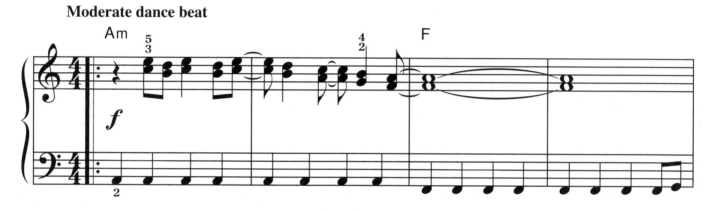

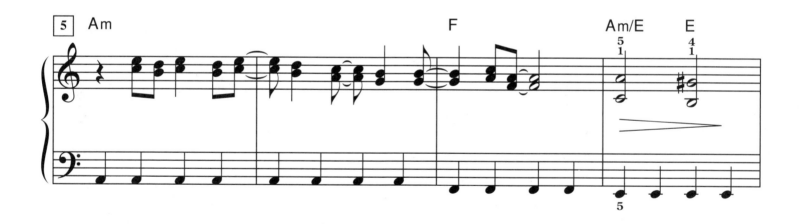

Verse:

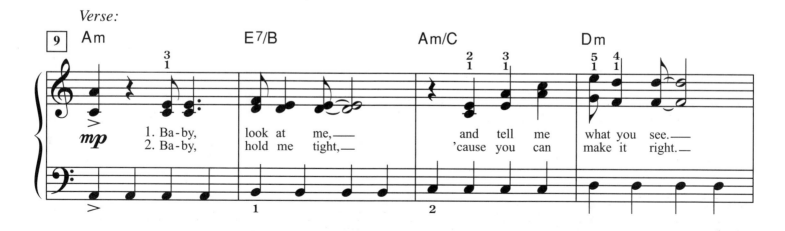

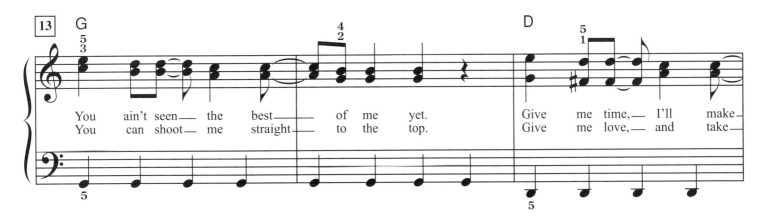

You ain't seen—— the best—— of me yet.
You can shoot—— me straight—— to the top.
Give me time,—— I'll make——
Give me love,—— and take——

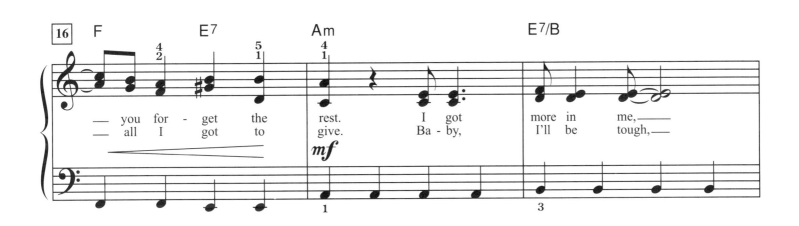

—— you for - get the rest. I got more in me,——
—— all I got to give. Ba - by, I'll be tough,——

mf

and you can set it free.—— I can catch—— the moon
too much is not e - nough.—— I can ride—— your heart

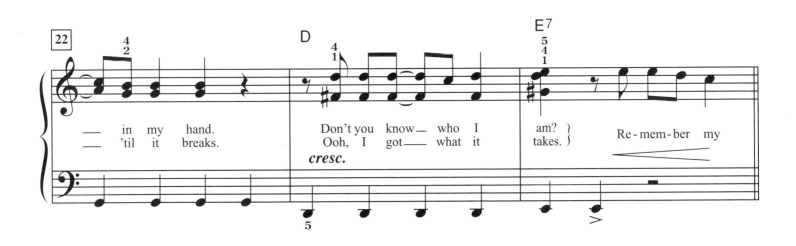

—— in my hand. Don't you know—— who I am? ⎫ Re - mem - ber my
—— 'til it breaks. Ooh, I got—— what it takes. ⎭

cresc.

Chorus:

name. Fame! I'm gon-na live—— for-ev - er.

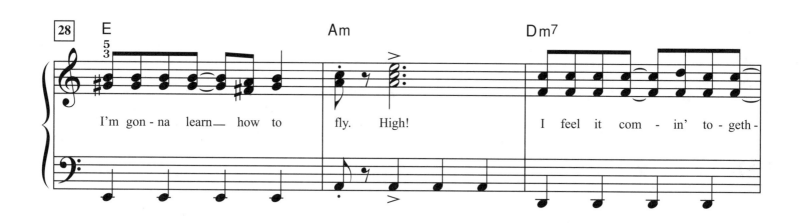

I'm gon-na learn—— how to fly. High! I feel it com - in' to-geth-

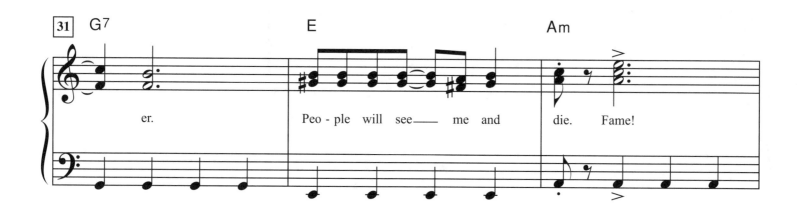

er. Peo - ple will see—— me and die. Fame!

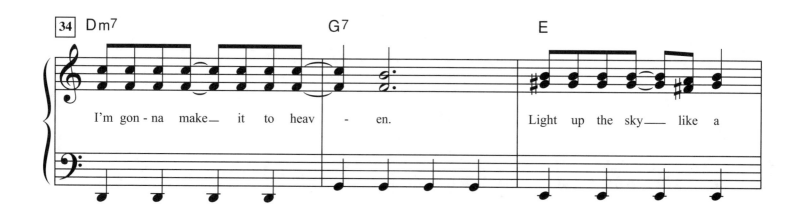

I'm gon-na make—— it to heav - en. Light up the sky—— like a

flame. Fame! I'm gon - na live___ for - ev - er.

Ba - by, re - mem - ber my name. Re - mem - ber, re - mem - ber, re - mem - ber, re - mem - ber.

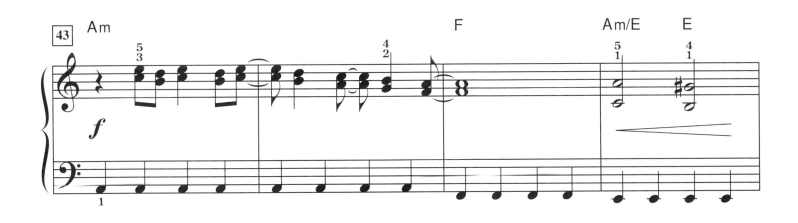

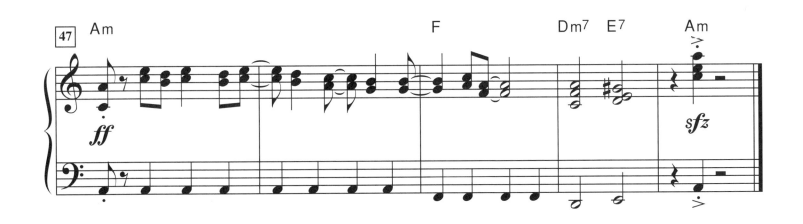

HEAVEN IS A PLACE ON EARTH

Belinda Carlisle began her career as the lead singer of the all-girl band The Go-Go's, the first all-female band in rock history to achieve a #1 album who also wrote their own music and played their own instruments. Their biggest hit was "We Got the Beat." Carlisle left the Go-Go's in 1985 for a solo career. She released "Heaven Is a Place on Earth" in 1987 which topped the Billboard Hot 100. Michelle Phillips of The Mamas and The Papas was one of the backup vocalists, and actress Diane Keaton directed the song's music video.

Words and Music by
Rick Nowels and Ellen Shipley
Arranged by Dan Coates

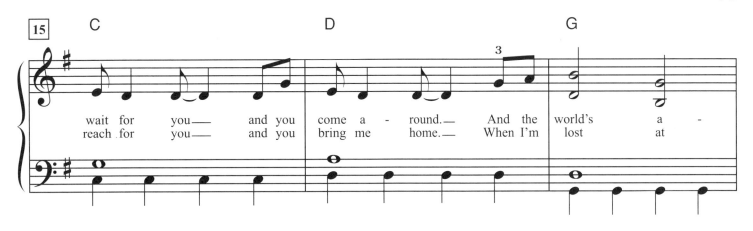

wait for you—— and you come a - round.—— And the world's a -
reach for you—— and you bring me home.—— When I'm lost at

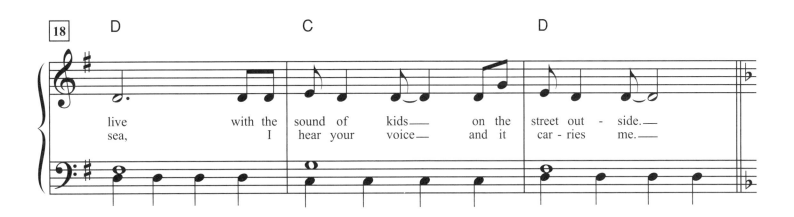

live with the sound of kids—— on the street out - side.——
sea, I hear your voice—— and it car - ries me.——

% *Bridge:*

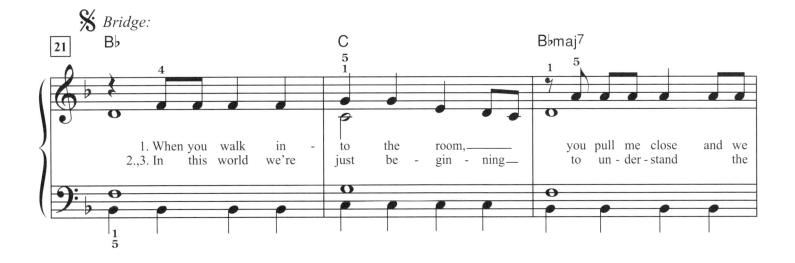

1. When you walk in - to the room,———— you pull me close and we
2.,3. In this world we're just be - gin - ning—— to un - der - stand the

start to move.—— And we're spin - ning with the stars a - bove and you
mir - a - cle of liv - ing. Ba - by, I—— was a - fraid be - fore but I'm

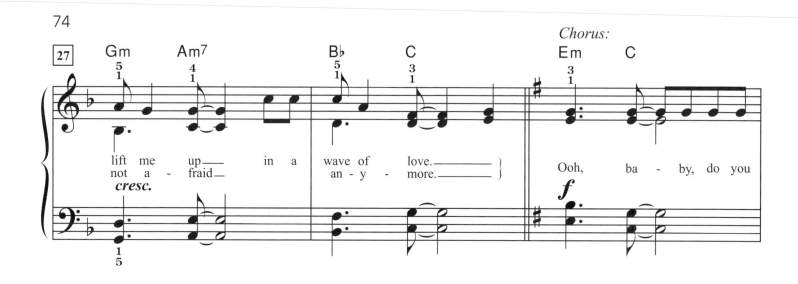

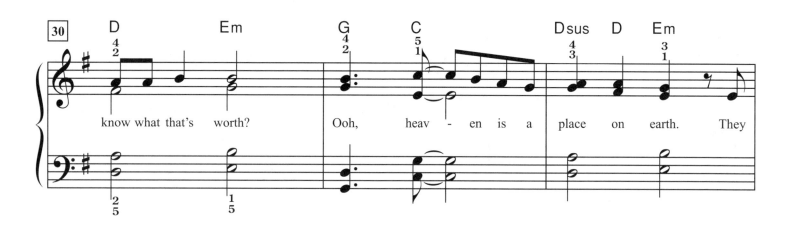

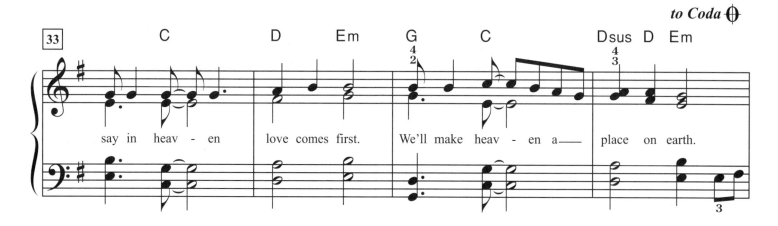

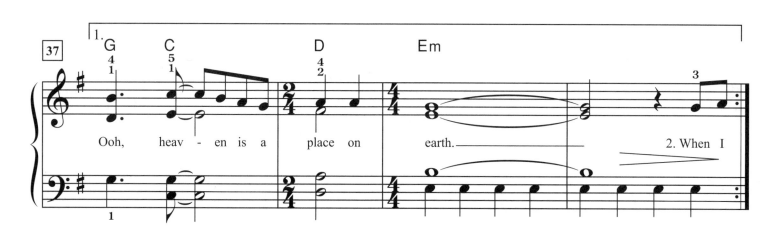

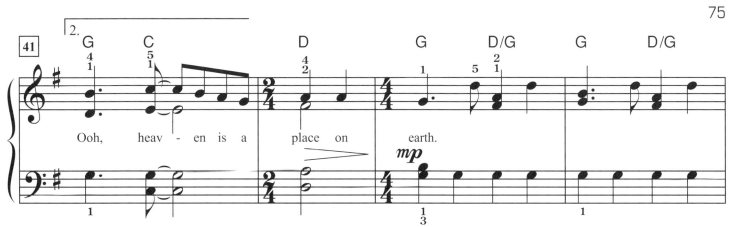

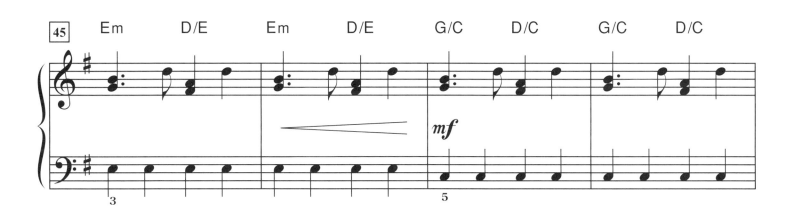

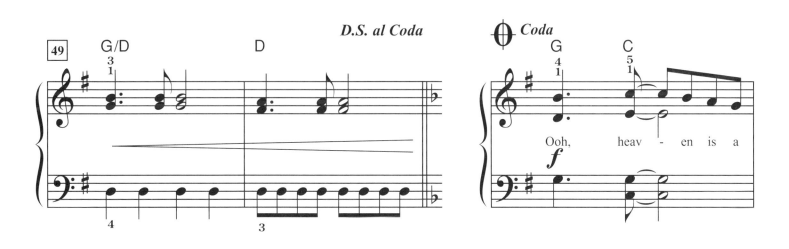

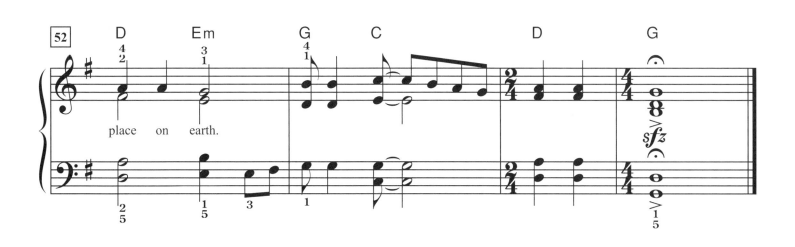

HOLD ON TO THE NIGHTS

Richard Marx's debut album *Richard Marx* (1988) yielded four hit singles and went three times platinum. With "Don't Mean Nothing," "Should've Known Better," "Endless Summer Nights," and "Hold On to the Nights" (which was his first #1 hit), Marx became the first male artist to have four singles from the same album in the top three spots in the charts. The album remained on the charts for more than a year and a half.

Words and Music by Richard Marx
Arranged by Dan Coates

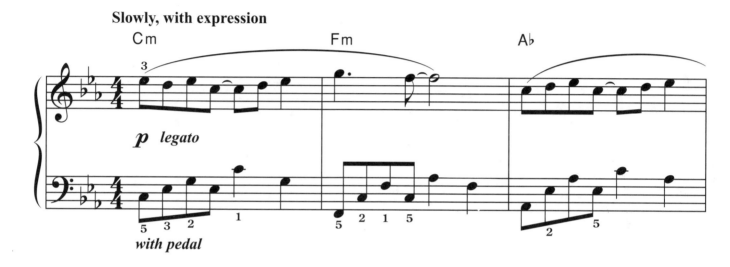

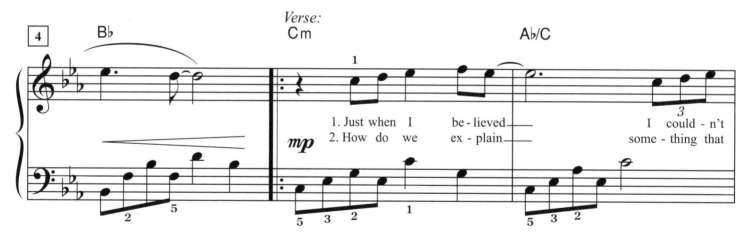

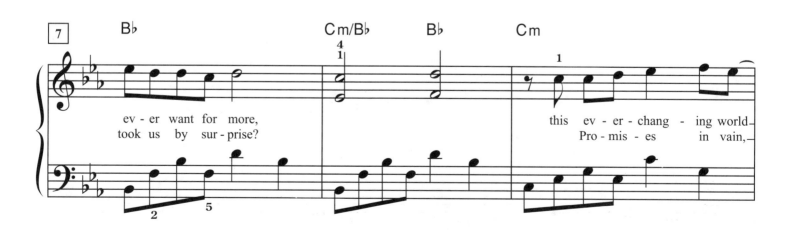

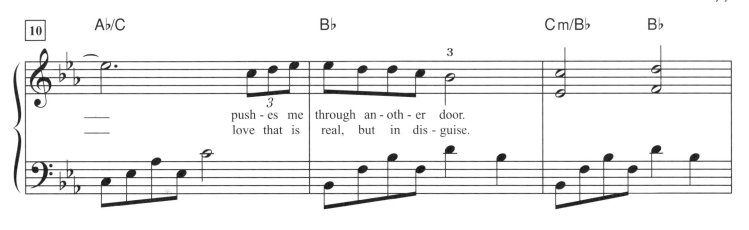

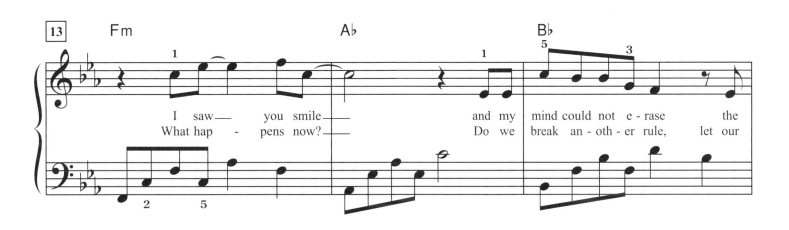

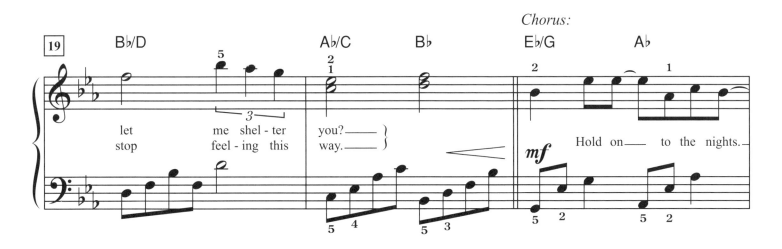

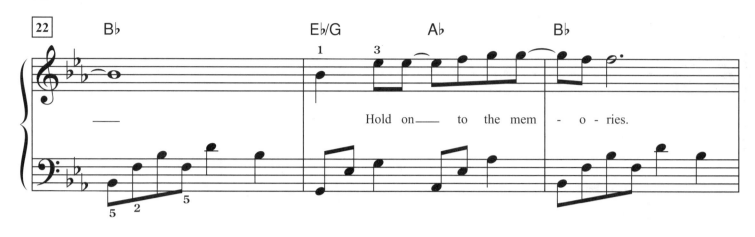

Hold on to the mem - o - ries.

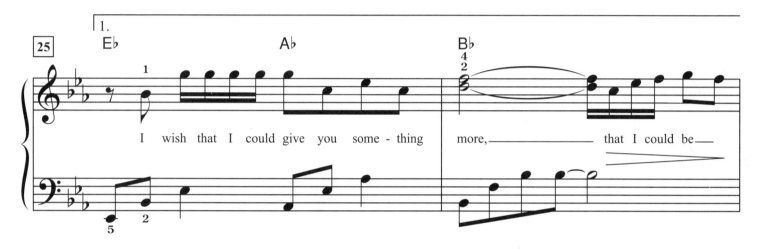

I wish that I could give you some - thing more, that I could be

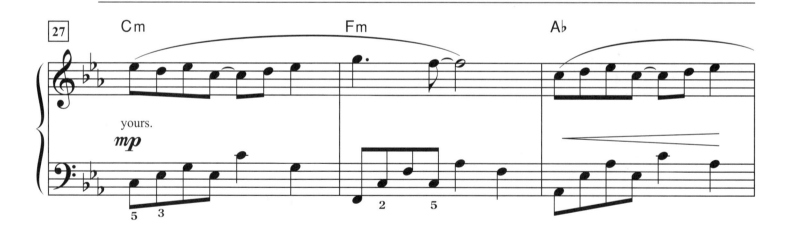

yours.

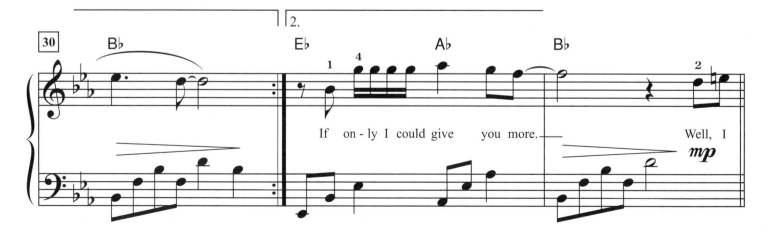

If on - ly I could give you more. Well, I

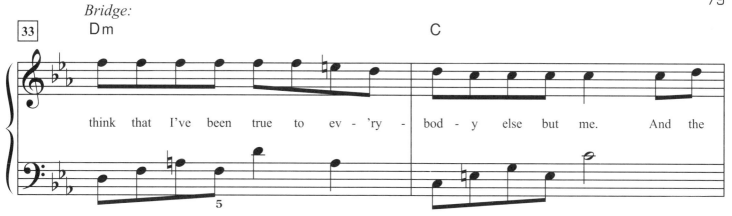

Bridge:

33 | **Dm** | **C**

think that I've been true to ev - 'ry - bod - y else but me. And the

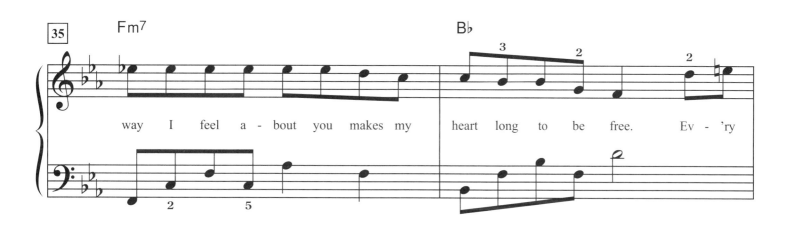

35 | **Fm7** | **B♭**

way I feel a - bout you makes my heart long to be free. Ev - 'ry

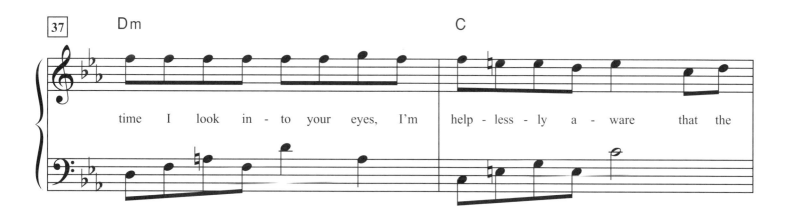

37 | **Dm** | **C**

time I look in - to your eyes, I'm help - less - ly a - ware that the

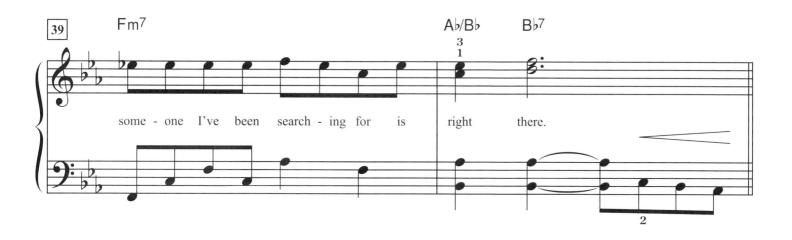

39 | **Fm7** | **A♭/B♭** | **B♭7**

some - one I've been search - ing for is right there.

IF I COULD TURN BACK TIME

"If I Could Turn Back Time" is from pop icon Cher's 20th album *Heart of Stone* (1989). It was Cher's second consecutive #1 hit on the Billboard Adult Contemporary chart following "After All" (on page 4) and was at the top of the charts in multiple countries. It has become one of Cher's signature songs alongside "Gypsys, Tramps & Thieves" (1971) and "Believe" (1998).

Words and Music by Diane Warren
Arranged by Dan Coates

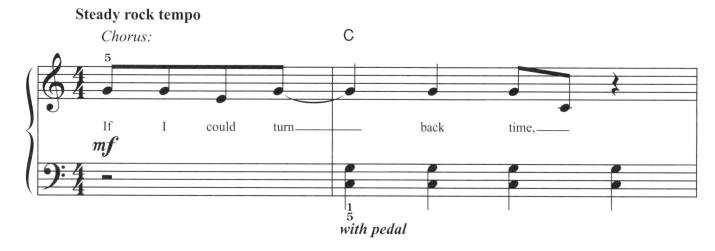

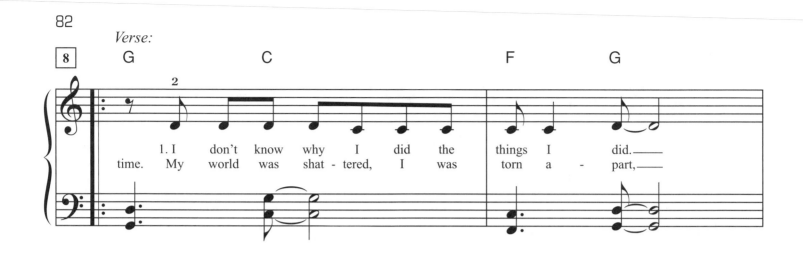

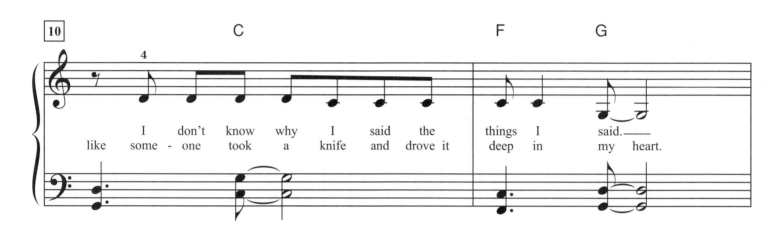

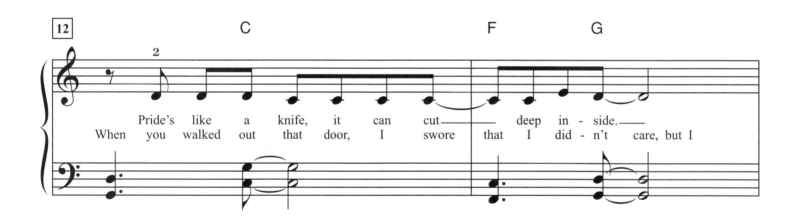

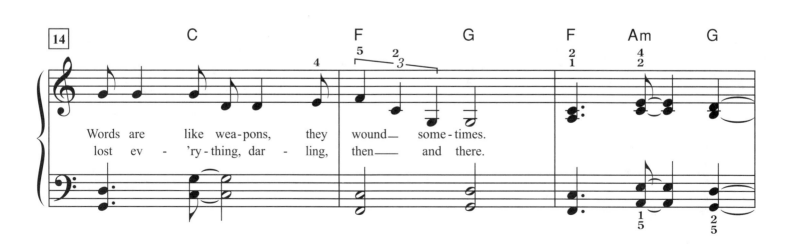

Chorus:

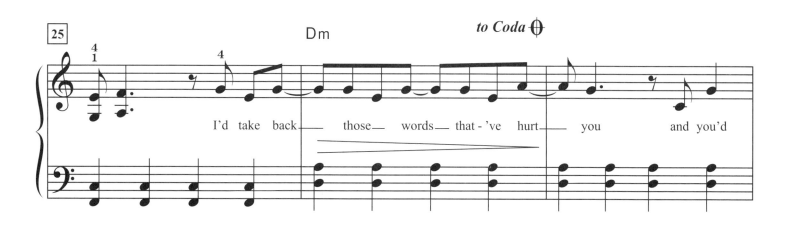

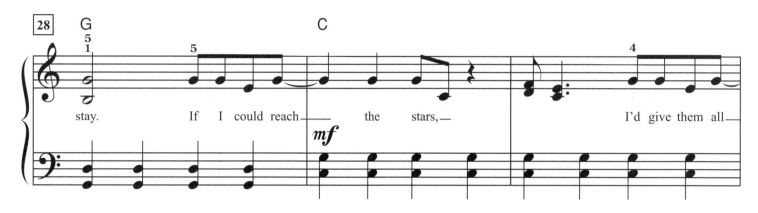

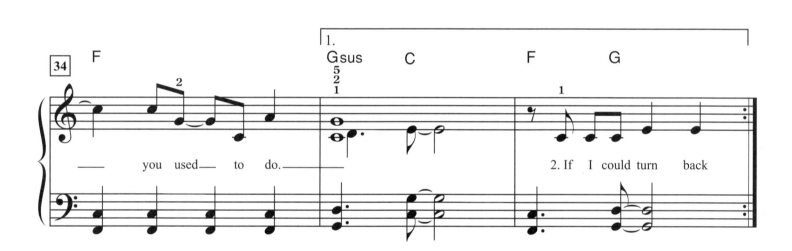

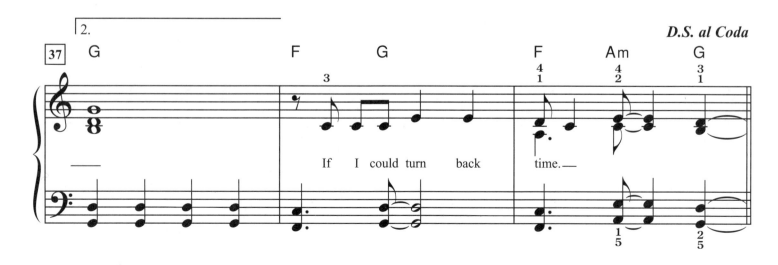

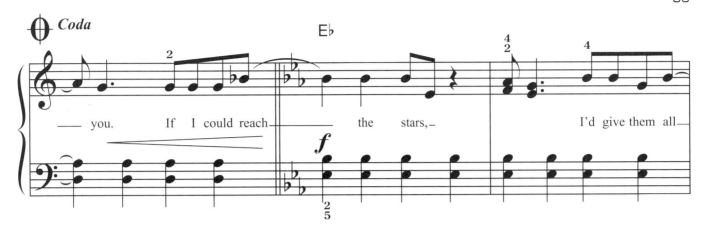

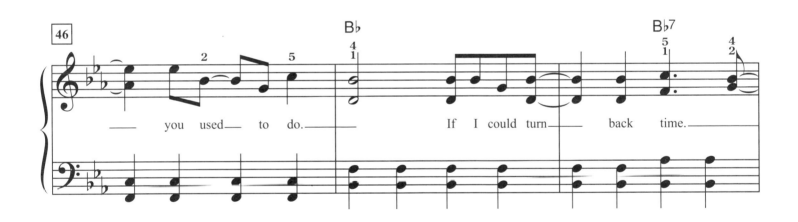

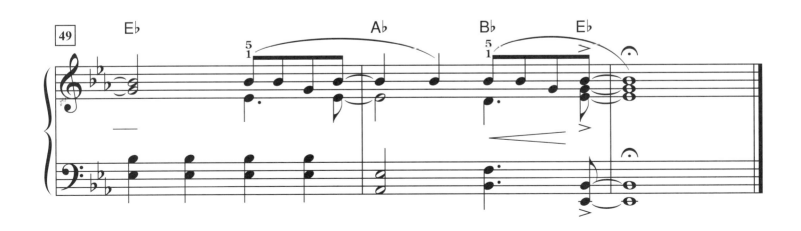

IS THIS LOVE

"Is This Love" is from rock band Survivor's sixth album *When Seconds Count* (1986). After the success of "Eye of the Tiger" (on page 60) in 1982, Survivor went through some hard times including a disappointing fourth album and the replacement of the lead singer. The band made a comeback with *Vital Signs* (which included the hit "The Search Is Over") and "Burning Heart" (the theme from *Rocky IV*). *When Seconds Count* continued this success streak and achieved gold record status.

Words and Music by
James Peterik and Frankie Sullivan III
Arranged by Dan Coates

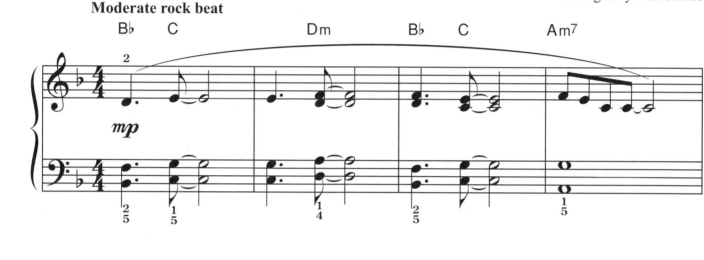

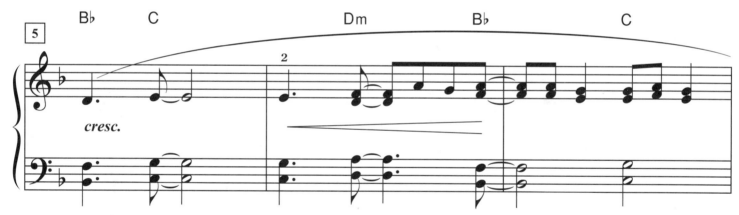

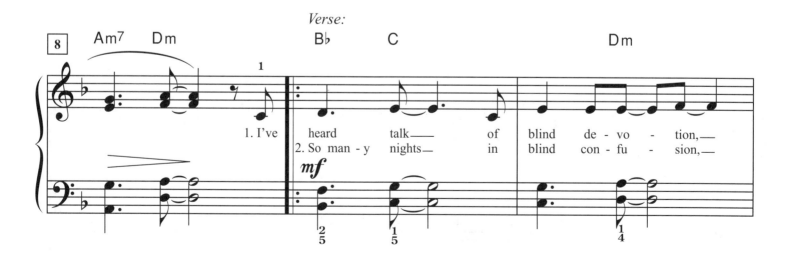

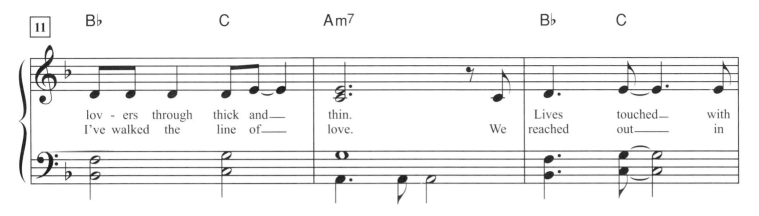

lov - ers through thick and— thin. We Lives touched— with
I've walked the line of— love. reached out— in

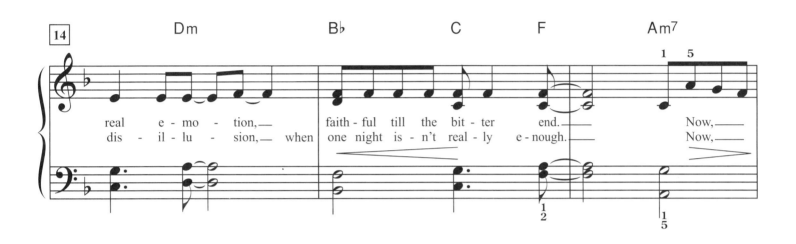

real e - mo - tion,— faith - ful till the bit - ter end. Now,—
dis - il - lu - sion,— when one night is - n't real - ly e - nough. Now,—

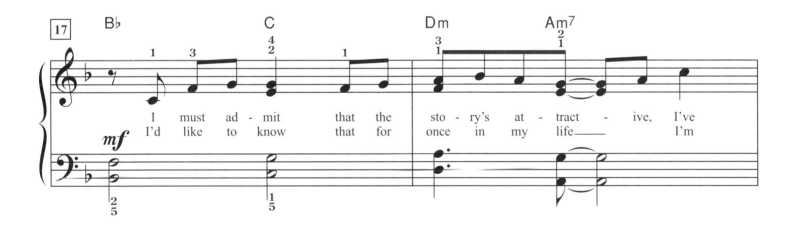

I must ad - mit that the sto - ry's at - tract - ive, I've
I'd like to know that for once in my life— I'm

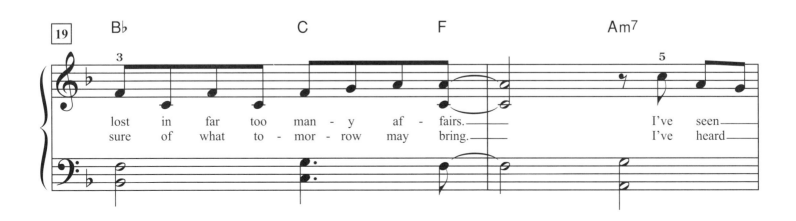

lost in far too man - y af - fairs. I've seen—
sure of what to - mor - row may bring. I've heard—

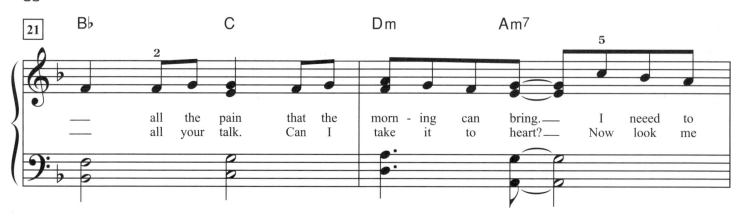

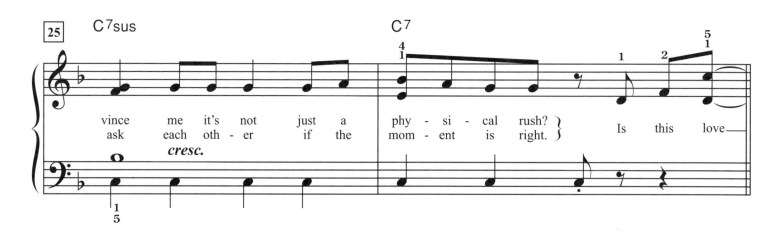

Chorus:

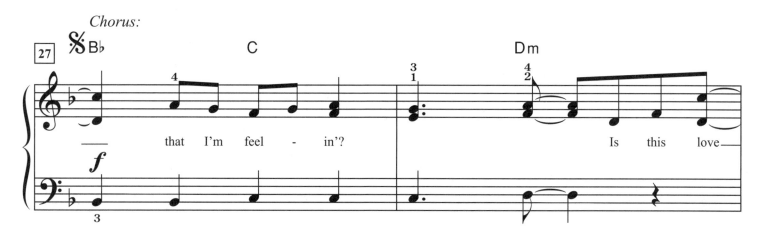

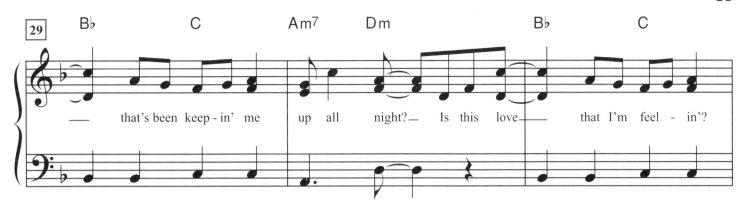

that's been keep-in' me up all night?— Is this love—— that I'm feel - in'?

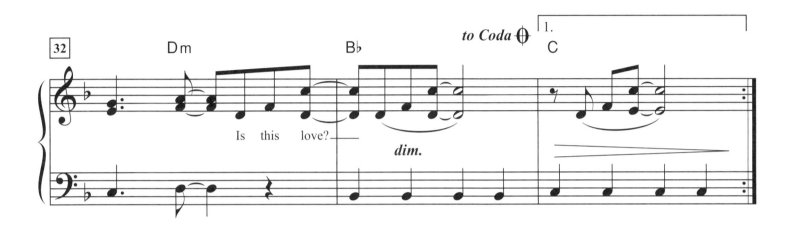

Is this love?—— *dim.*

to Coda

Is this love? that I'm feel-in'?

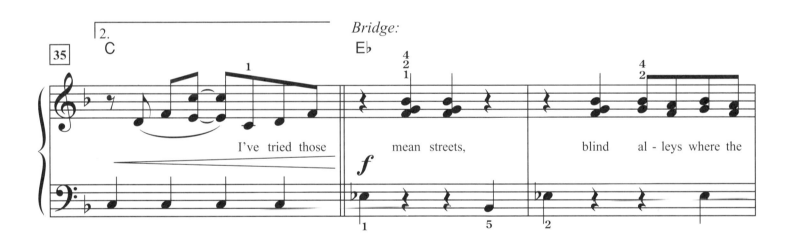

Bridge:

I've tried those mean streets, blind al - leys where the

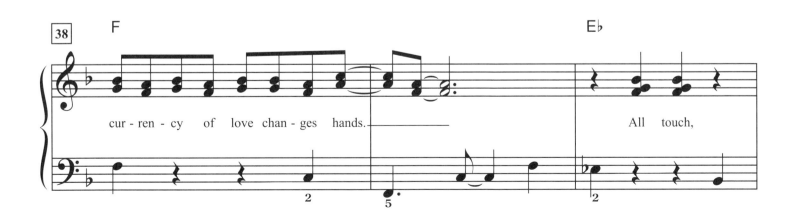

cur - ren - cy of love chan - ges hands. All touch,

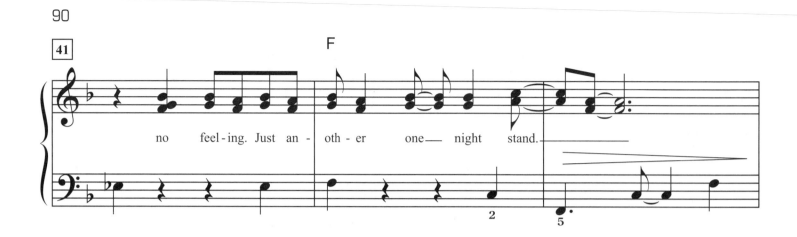

no feel-ing. Just an - oth - er one—— night stand.——

I need to know that there's some-one who cares.— Could you be the an - gel to

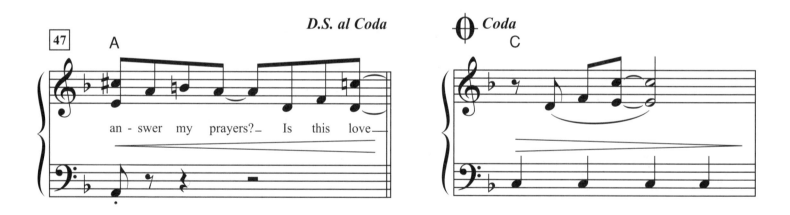

D.S. al Coda

Coda

an - swer my prayers?— Is this love—

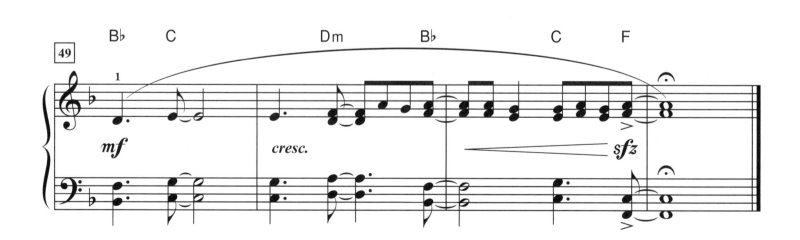

MORNING TRAIN
(NINE TO FIVE)

Sheena Easton recorded "9 to 5" in 1980. The title was changed to "Morning Train (Nine to Five)" for its North American release to avoid confusion with the Dolly Parton song of the same name. Easton's single became her first and greatest major hit, topping the Billboard Hot 100. Easton, a native of Scotland, was discovered on a 1980 U.K. reality TV show (*The Big Time*) which chronicled her successful attempts at gaining a recording contract. In addition to singing, Easton is also a successful songwriter and actress.

Words and Music by Florrie Palmer
Arranged by Dan Coates

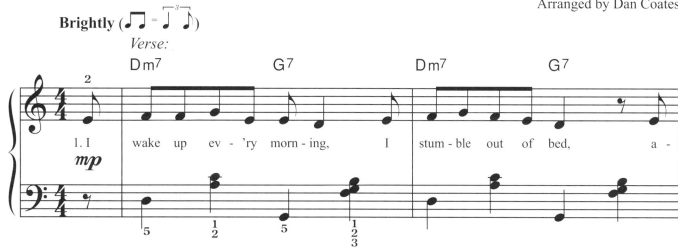

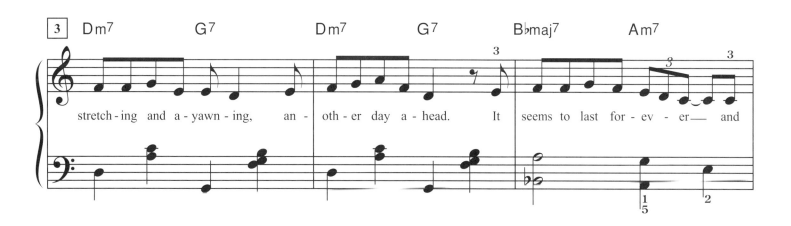

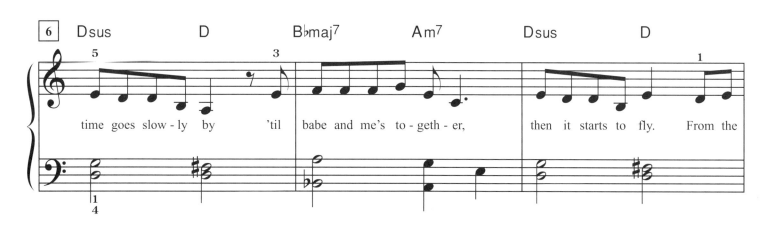

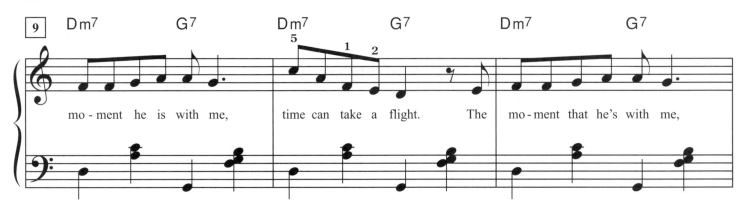

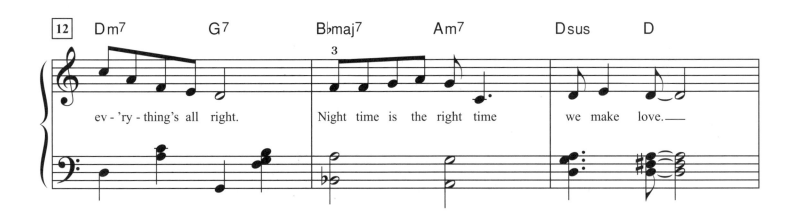

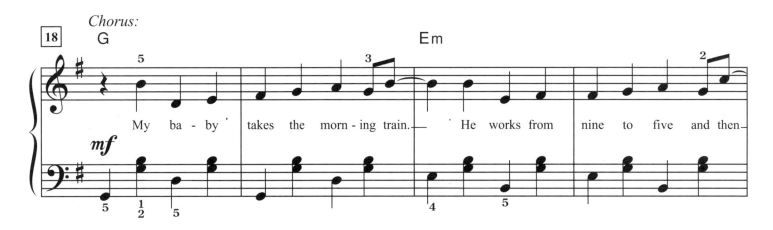

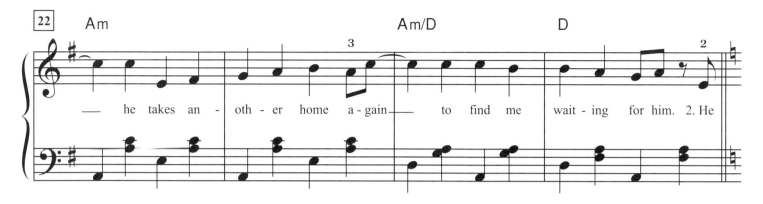

he takes an - oth - er home a - gain to find me wait - ing for him. 2. He

Verse:

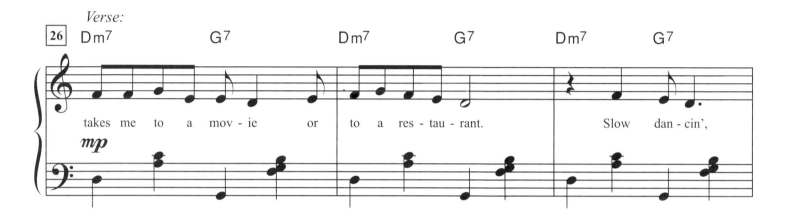

takes me to a mov - ie or to a res - tau - rant. Slow dan - cin',

mp

an - y - thing I want. On - ly when he's with me, I catch a light.

On - ly what he gives me makes me feel all right.

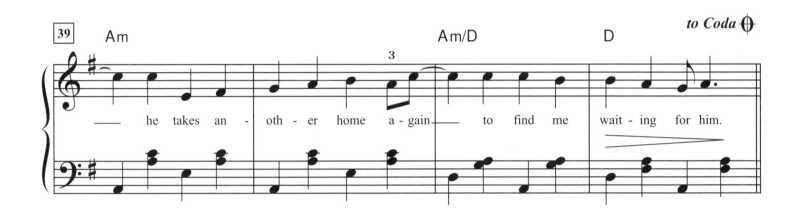

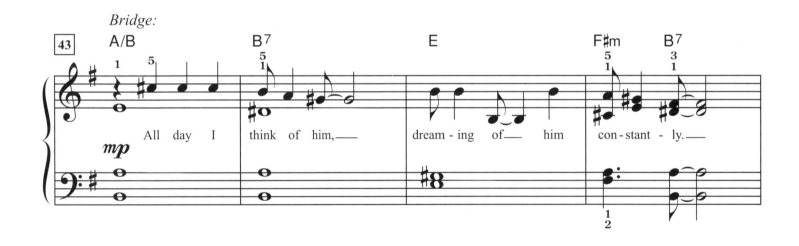

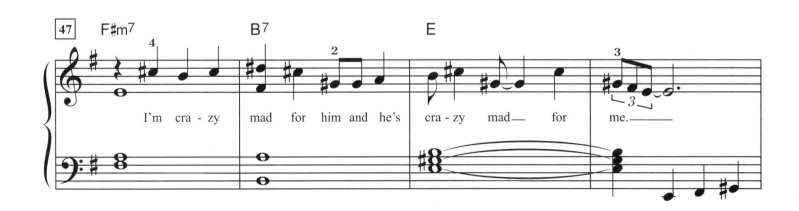

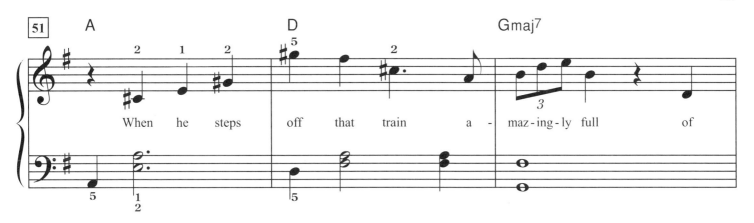

When he steps off that train a - maz-ing-ly full of

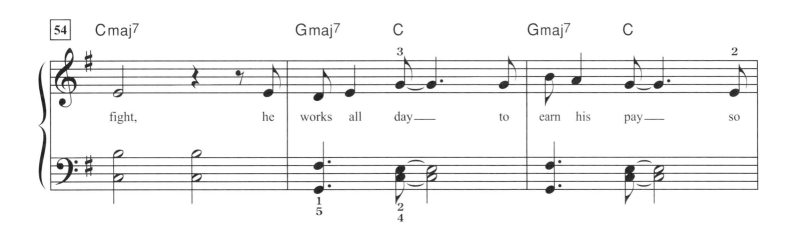

fight, he works all day to earn his pay so

we can play all night.

D.S. al Coda

Coda

mf

rit.

OPEN ARMS

Journey, a San Francisco-based rock band which formed in 1973, was at the height of their career when they recorded "Open Arms" in 1982. The single is from their seventh studio album, *Escape*, which has become their biggest selling and most popular album which has gone nine times platinum. "Open Arms" spent six weeks at #2 on the Billboard Hot 100 and was voted #1 on VH1's "25 Greatest Power Ballads" list.

Words and Music by
Steve Perry and Jonathan Cain
Arranged by Dan Coates

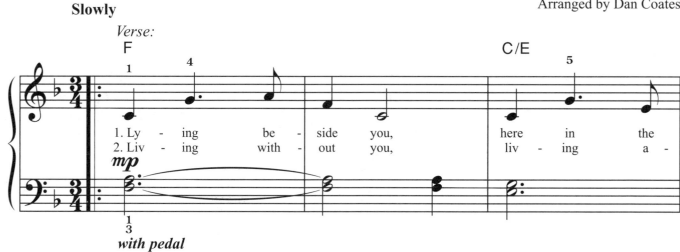

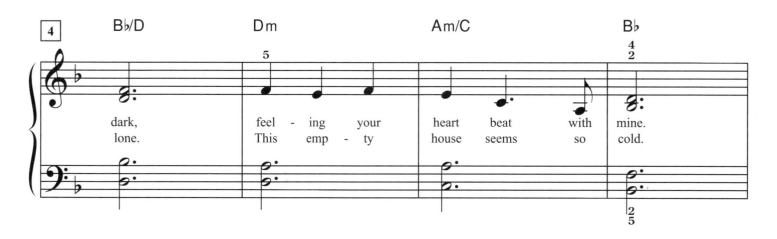

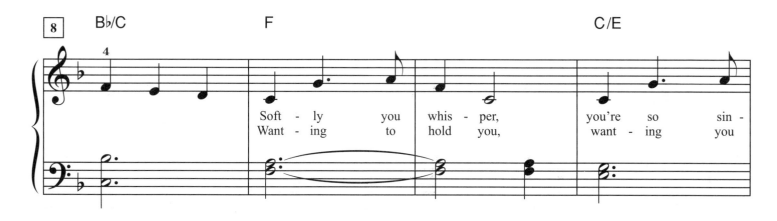

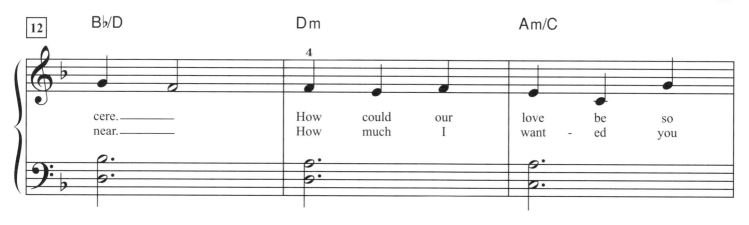

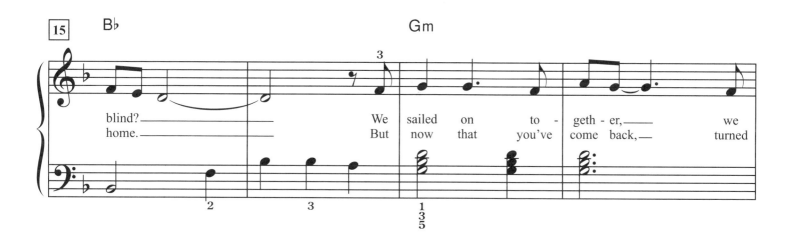

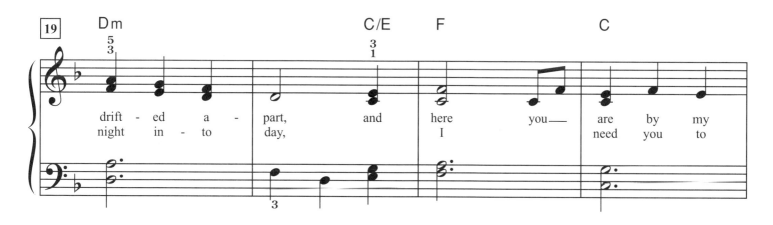

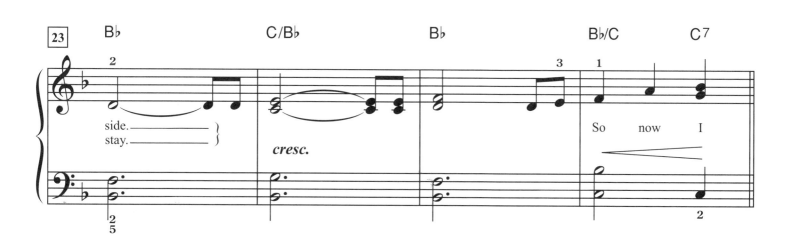

Chorus:

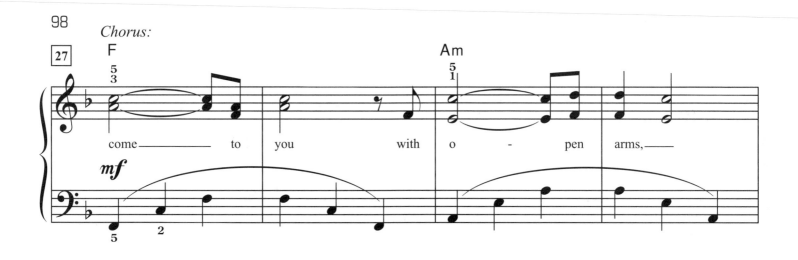

come ———— to you with o - pen arms, ———

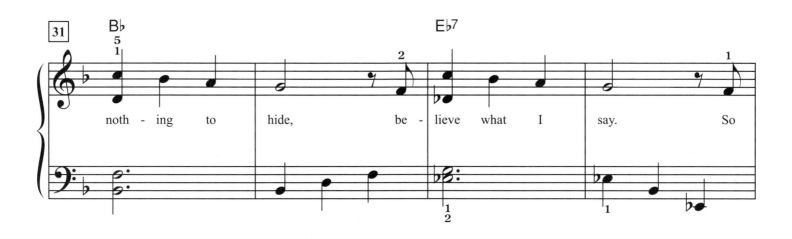

noth - ing to hide, be - lieve what I say. So

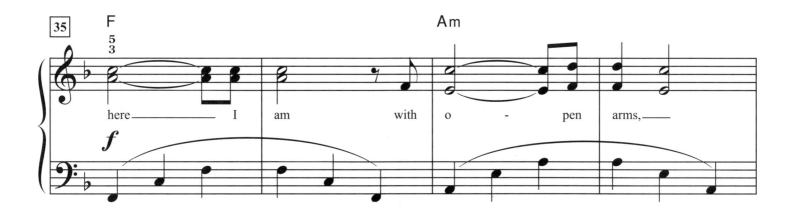

here ———— I am with o - pen arms, ———

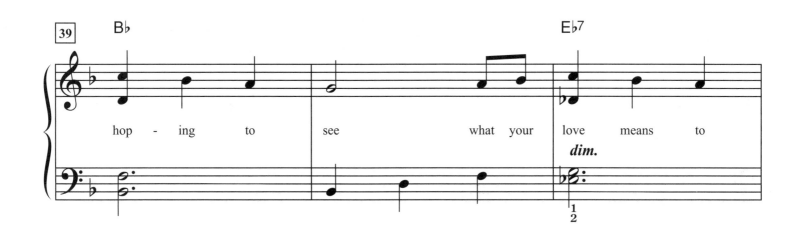

hop - ing to see what your love means to

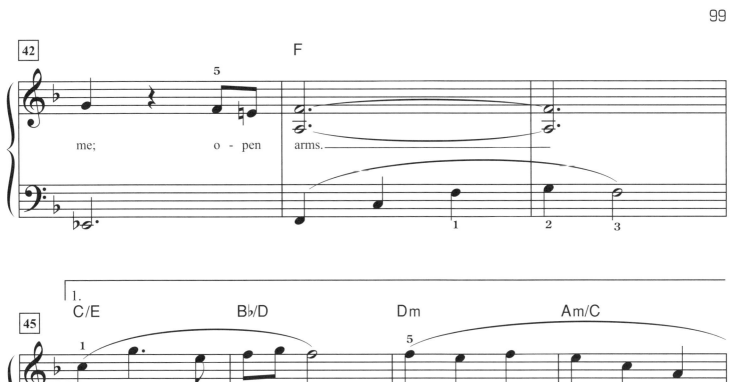

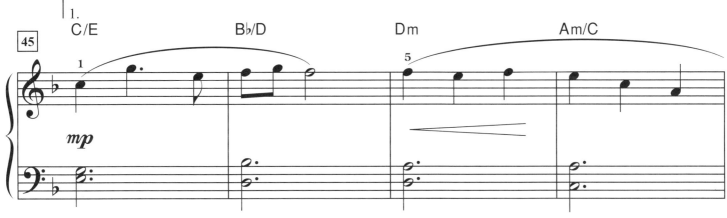

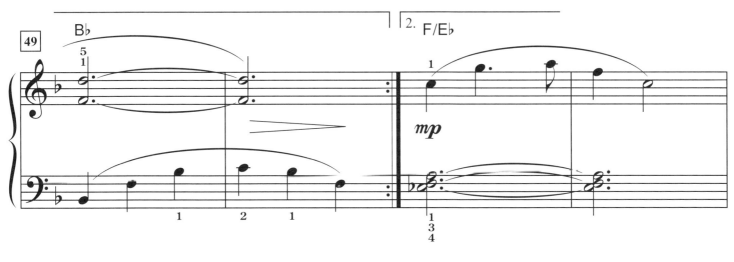

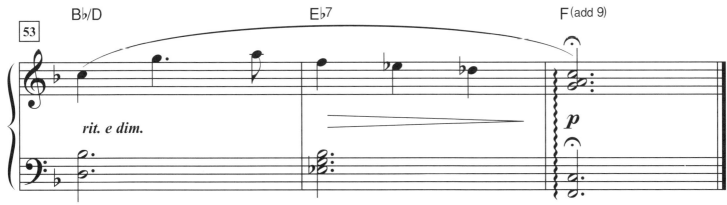

PIANO IN THE DARK

Brenda Russell's biggest hit "Piano in the Dark" is from her 1988 album *Get Here* which she started working on after moving to Sweden in the mid-'80s. In addition to her solo singing, Russell's dynamic career includes film scoring (*How Stella Got Her Groove Back*, 1998) and scoring for Broadway (*The Color Purple*, 2007).

Words and Music by
Brenda Russell, Jeff Hull and Scott Cutler
Arranged by Dan Coates

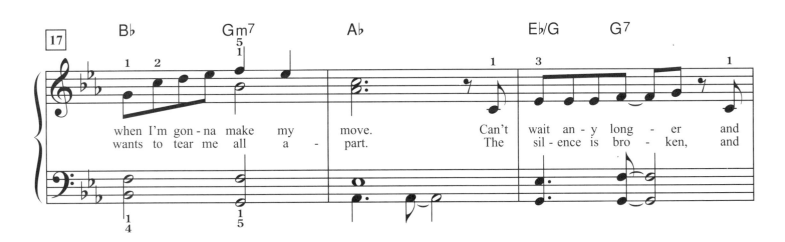

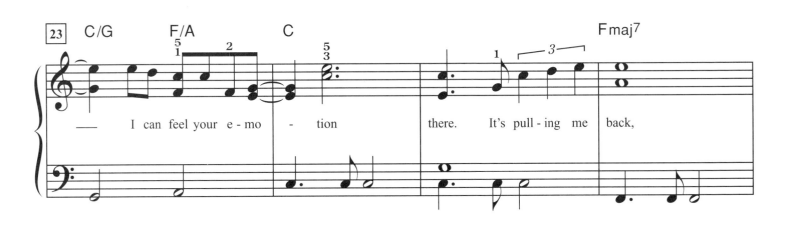

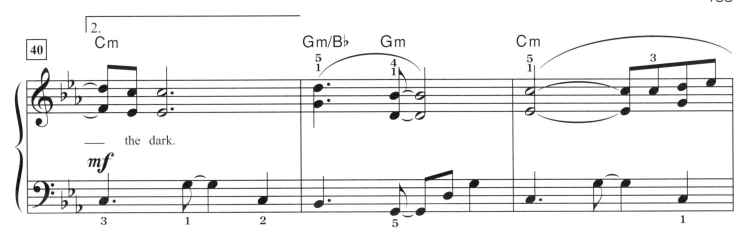

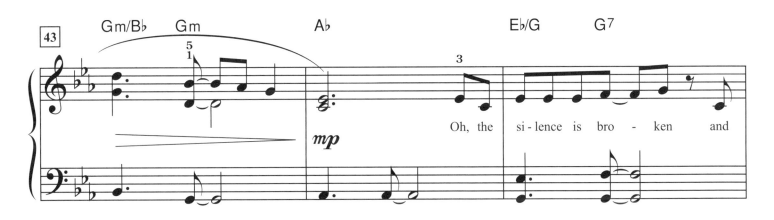

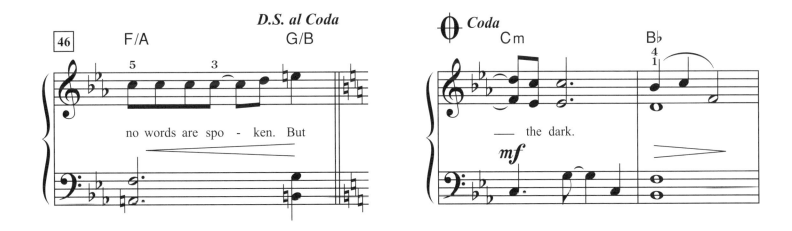

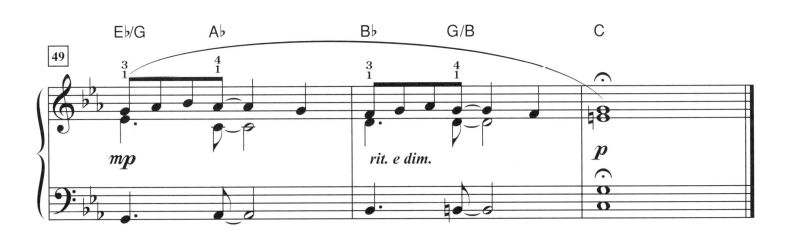

RIGHT HERE WAITING FOR YOU

"Right Here Waiting for You" is the second single (after "Satisfied") from Richard Marx's second album *Repeat Offender* (1989). Marx wrote most of the music for *Repeat Offender* while on his 14-month world tour promoting his self-titled first album. "Right Here Waiting for You" peaked at #1 on the Billboard Hot 100 and stayed there for three weeks.

Words and Music by Richard Marx
Arranged by Dan Coates

Moderately, with expression

Verse:

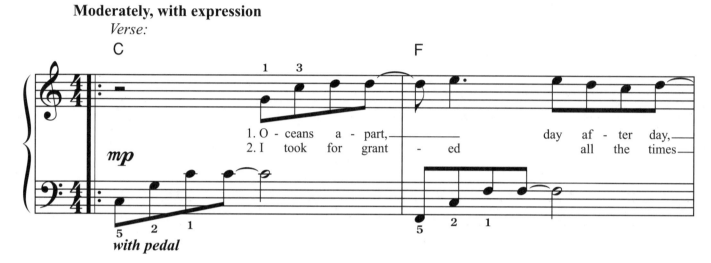

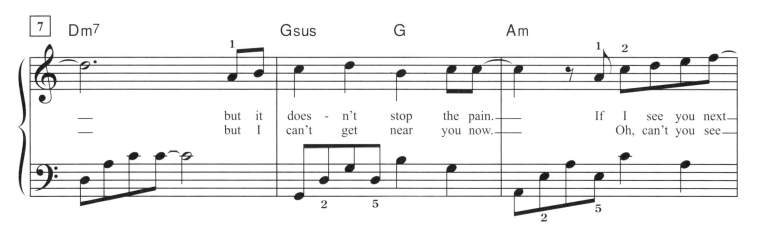

7 Dm7   Gsus   G   Am

but it does - n't stop the pain. If I see you next
but I can't get near you now. Oh, can't you see

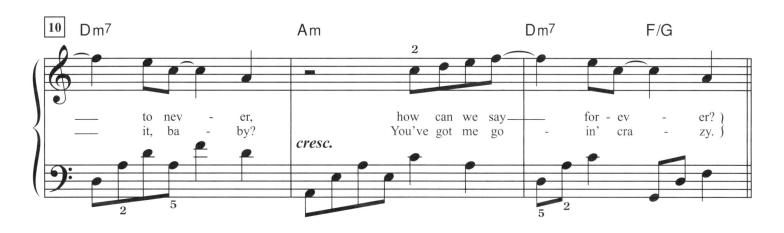

10 Dm7   Am   Dm7   F/G

to nev - er, how can we say for - ev - er?
it, ba - by? You've got me go - in' cra - zy.

cresc.

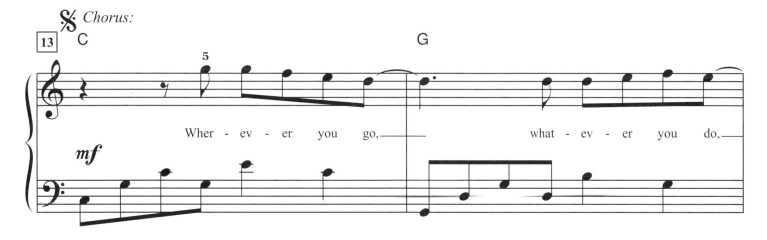

Chorus:

13 C   G

Wher - ev - er you go, what - ev - er you do,

mf

15 Am   F   G

I will be right here wait - ing for you.

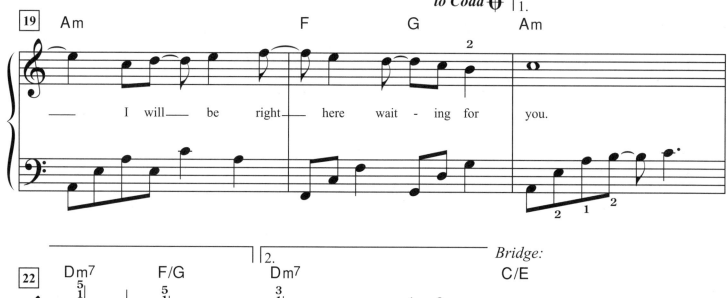

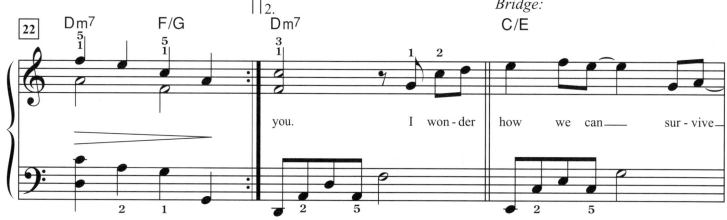

D.S. al Coda

end, if I'm with you, I'll take the chance.

you.

mp

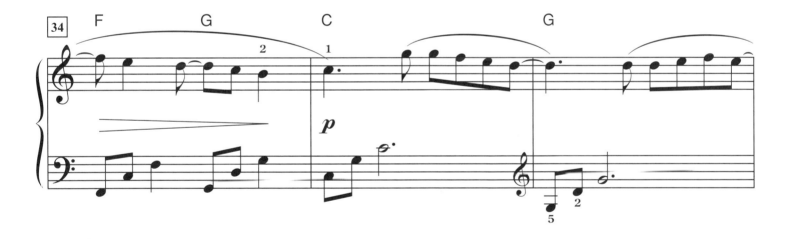

p

rit. e dim.

pp

TAKE MY BREATH AWAY

The new wave band Berlin formed in Orange County, California, in the late '70s. Their first single "The Metro" is a prime example of the new wave genre—blending punk, pop, and cutting-edge synthesizer technology. The band recorded the love song "Take My Breath Away" for *Top Gun*, the 1986 fighter pilot film starring Tom Cruise, Kelly McGillis, and Val Kilmer. The song reached #1 on the Billboard Hot 100 and won an Academy Award and a Golden Globe Award for Best Original Song.

Music by Giorgio Moroder
Words by Tom Whitlock
Arranged by Dan Coates

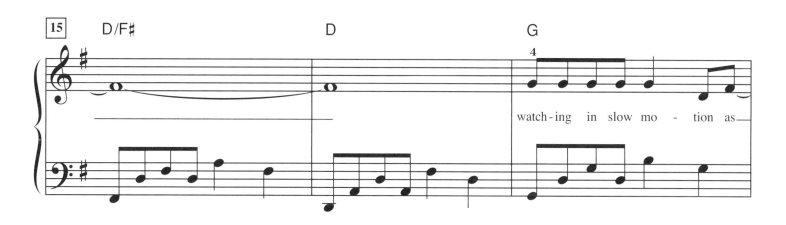

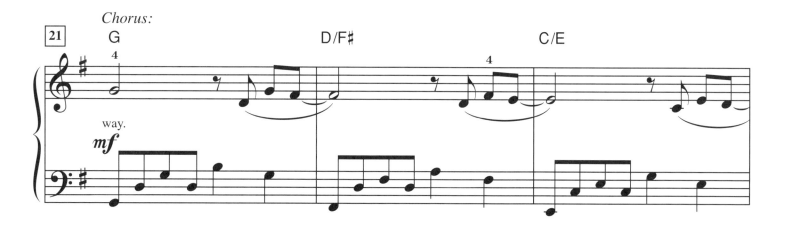

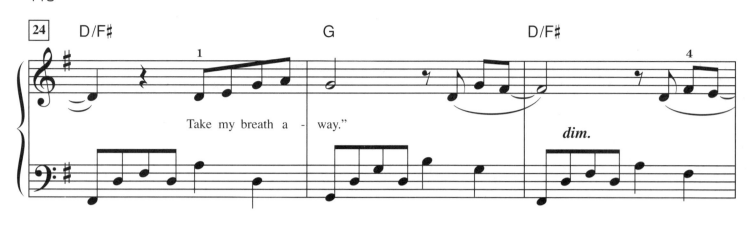

Take my breath a - way."

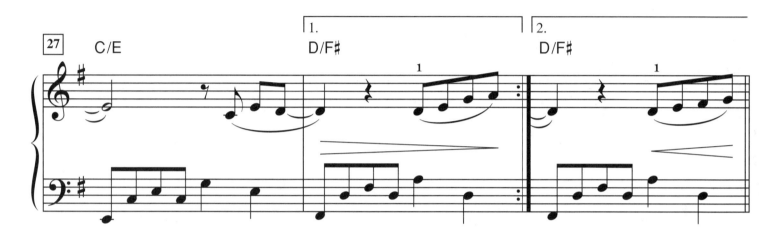

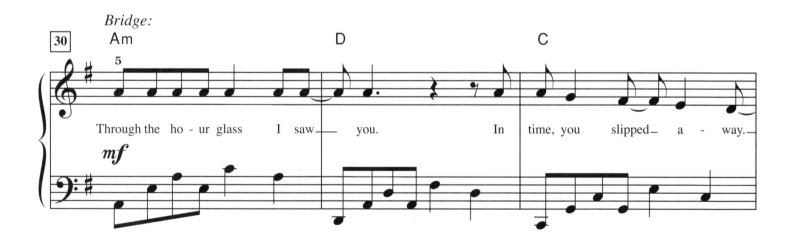

Through the ho - ur glass I saw you. In time, you slipped a - way.

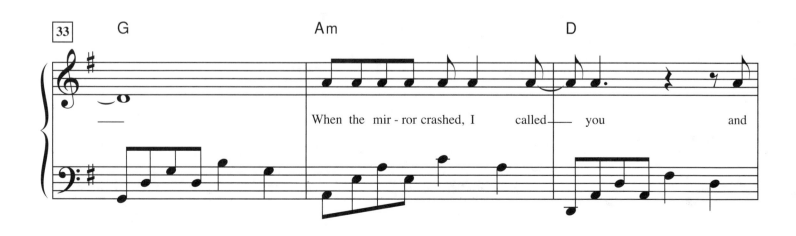

When the mir - ror crashed, I called you and

THAT'S WHAT FRIENDS ARE FOR

"That's What Friends Are For" was originally recorded by Rod Stewart as the closing theme music for the 1982 comedy *Night Shift*, director Ron Howard's first big budget film. The better known cover version of the song is by Dionne Warwick and a group of her superstar vocalist friends—Elton John, Gladys Knight, and Stevie Wonder. The cover was released in 1985 as a charity single and raised over 3 million dollars for the American Foundation for AIDS Research. It was *Billboard Magazine*'s #1 single of 1986.

Music by Burt Bacharach
Words by Carole Bayer Sager
Arranged by Dan Coates

Moderately slow, in two

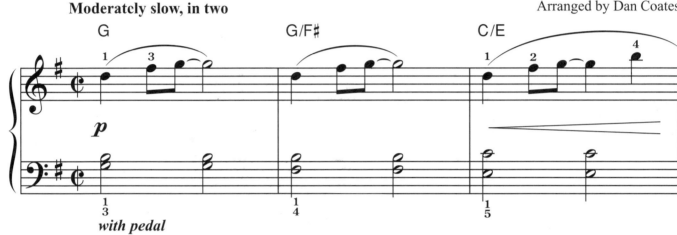

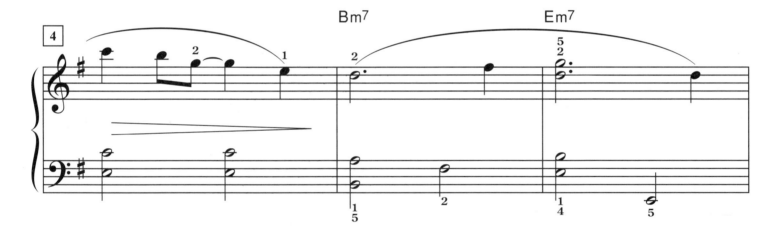

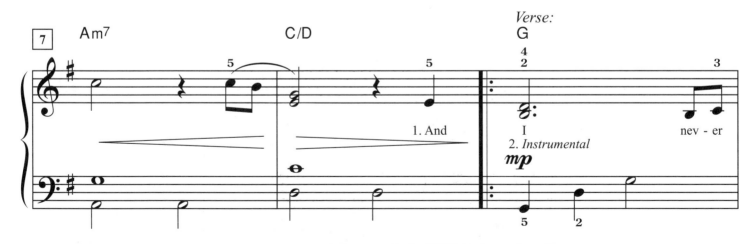

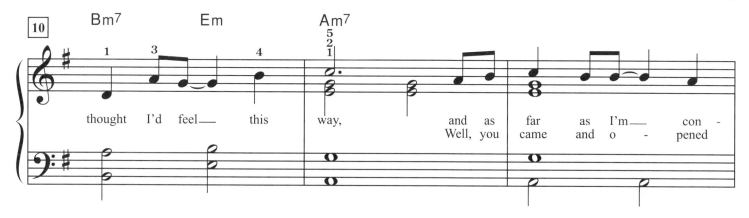

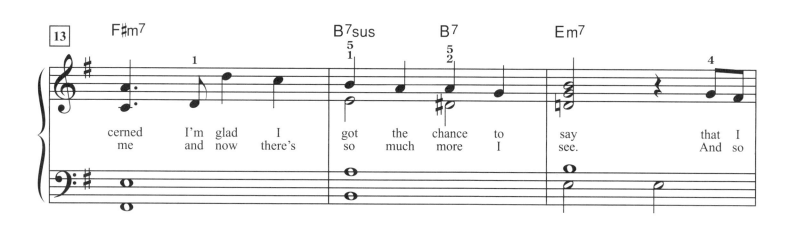

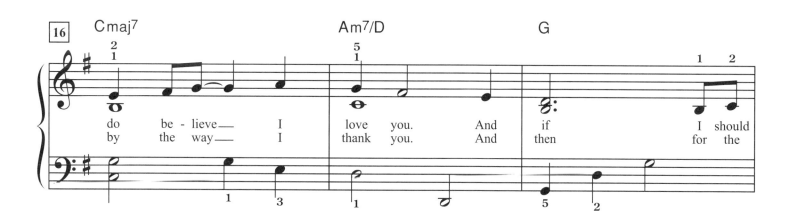

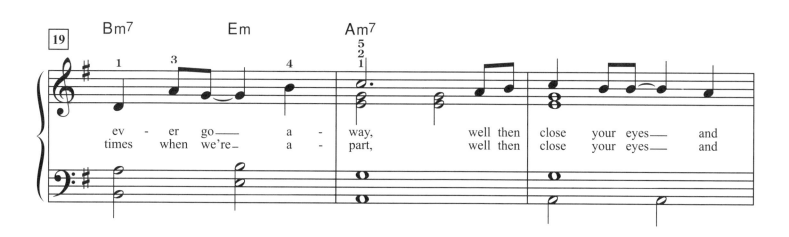

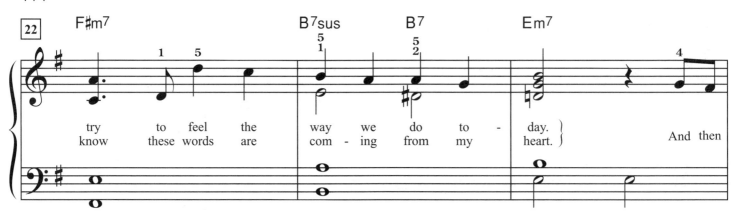

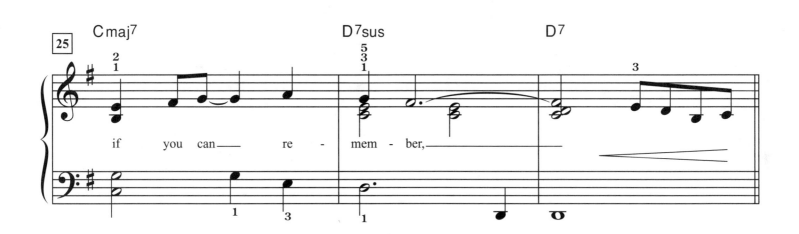

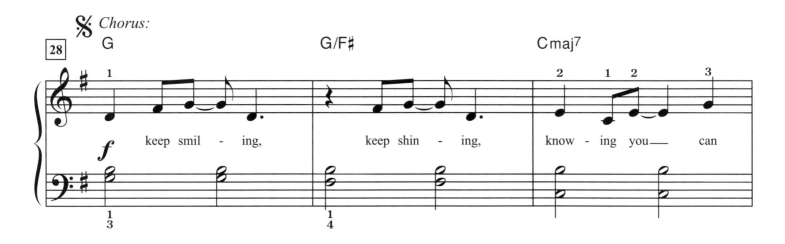

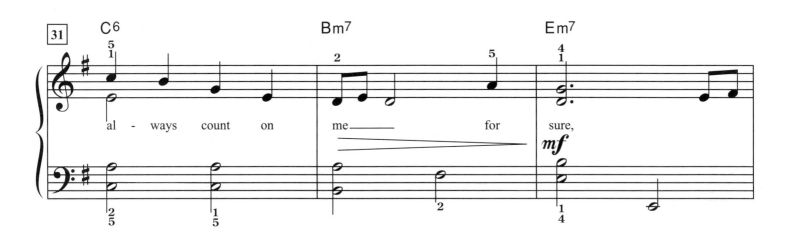

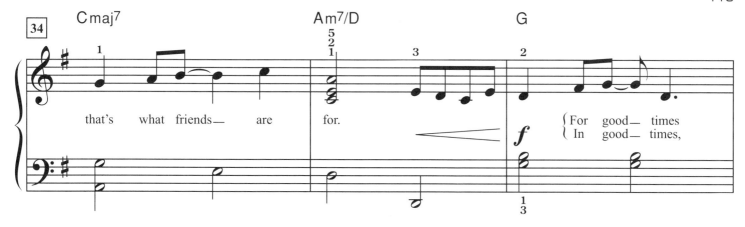

34 Cmaj7 / Am7/D / G

that's what friends— are for.
For good— times
In good— times,

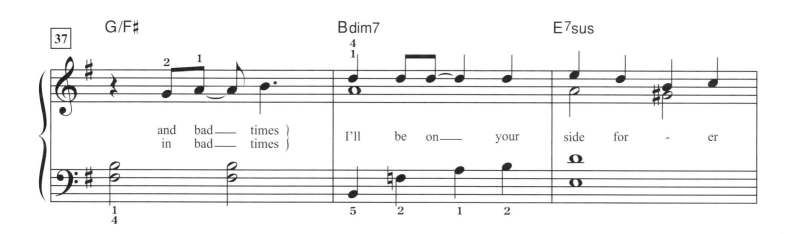

37 G/F# / Bdim7 / E7sus

and bad— times
in bad— times
I'll be on— your side for - er

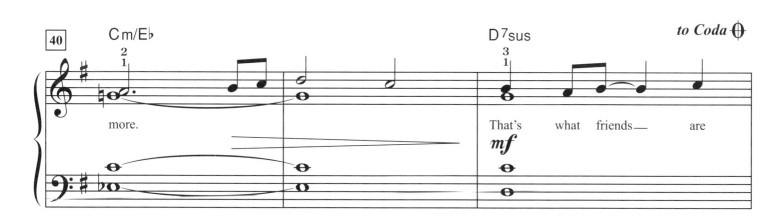

40 Cm/E♭ / D7sus / *to Coda* ⊕

more.
That's what friends— are

mf

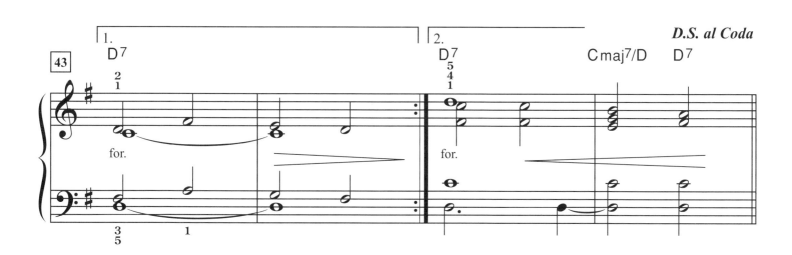

1. D7 / 2. D7 / Cmaj7/D D7 / *D.S. al Coda*

43

for.
for.

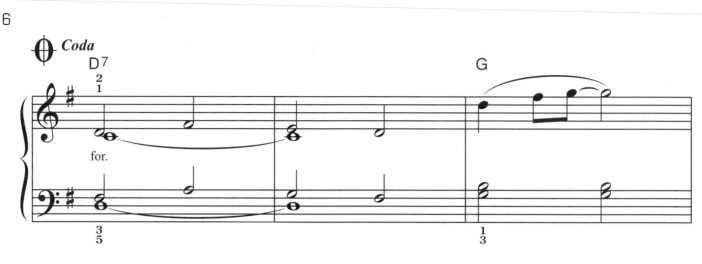

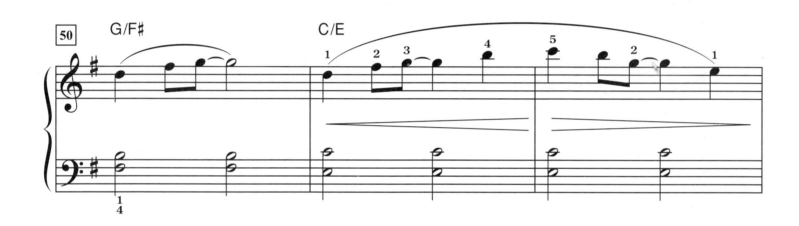

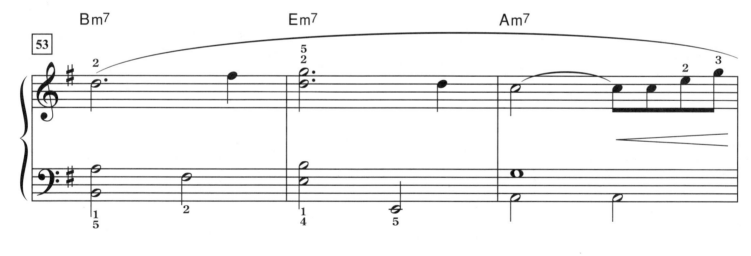

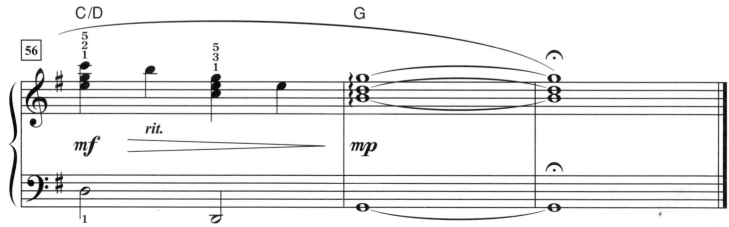

WE ARE THE WORLD

"We Are the World" was written in 1985 by Michael Jackson and Lionel Richie as a fundraising song to help provide relief for famine-stricken Ethiopia which had experienced unusual drought in 1984–85. USA for Africa (United Support of Artists for Africa) was a supergroup of musicians who recorded the song including Ray Charles, Bob Dylan, Michael Jackson, Billy Joel, Cyndi Lauper, Bette Midler, Willie Nelson, Lionel Richie, Smokey Robinson, Diana Ross, Paul Simon, Bruce Springsteen, Tina Turner, Dionne Warwick, Stevie Wonder, and many others. The song won four Grammy Awards and raised over $63 million.

Words and Music by
Michael Jackson and Lionel Richie
Arranged by Dan Coates

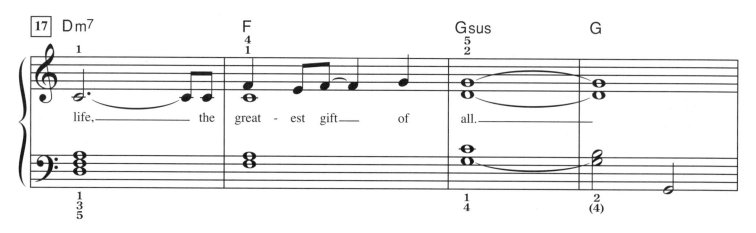

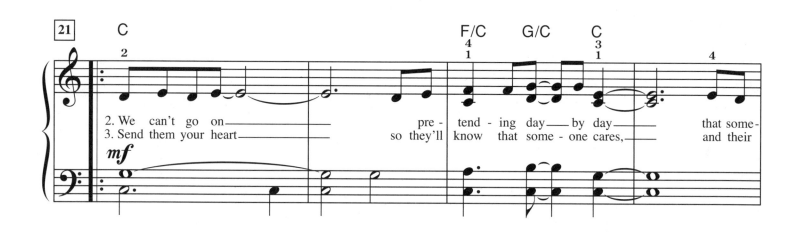

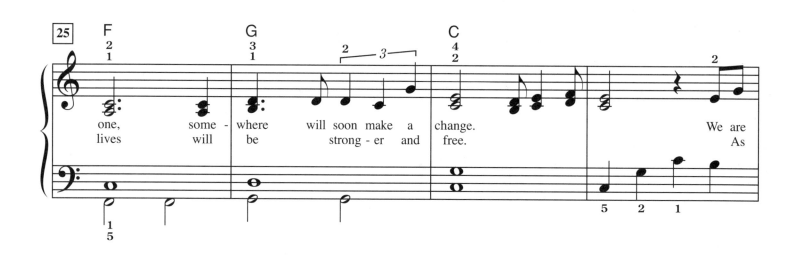

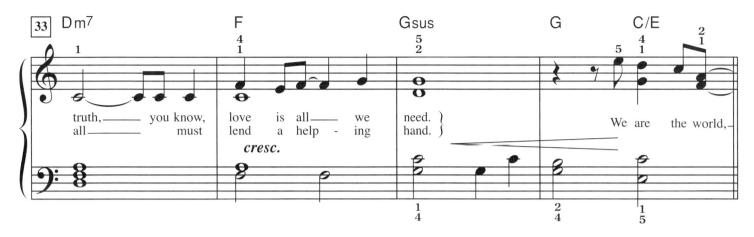

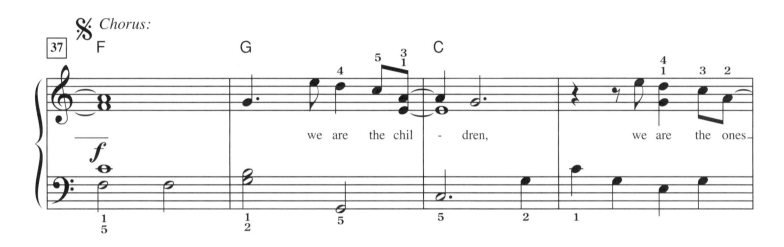

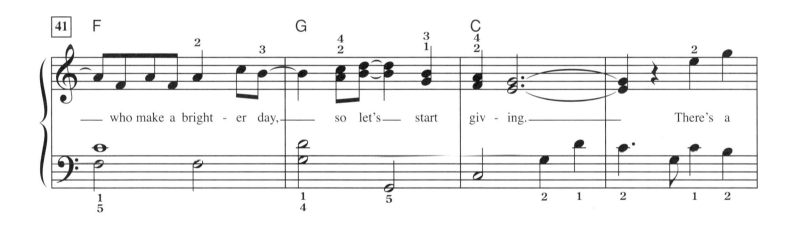

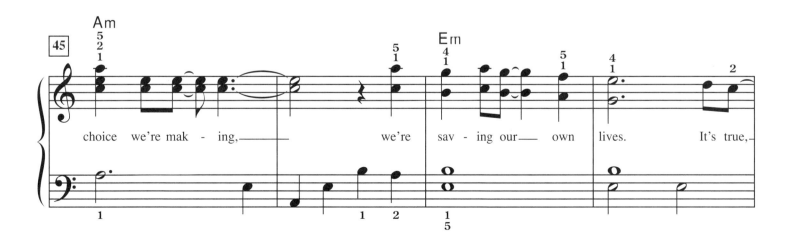

120

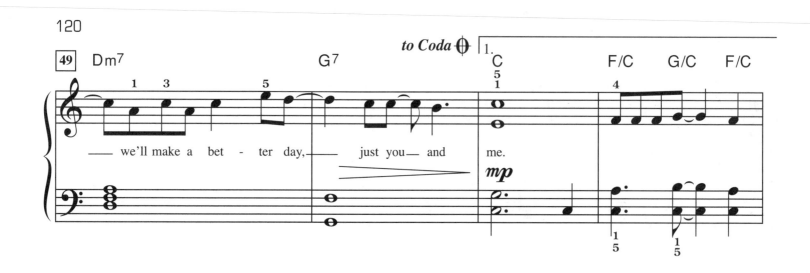

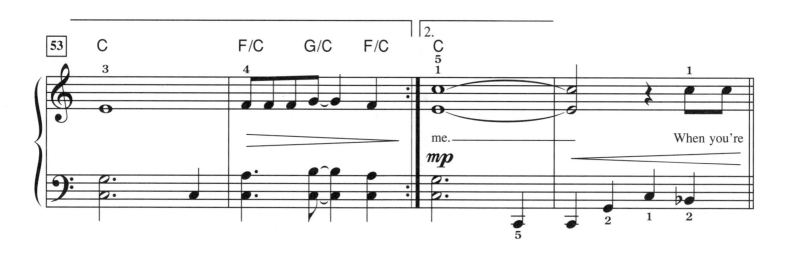

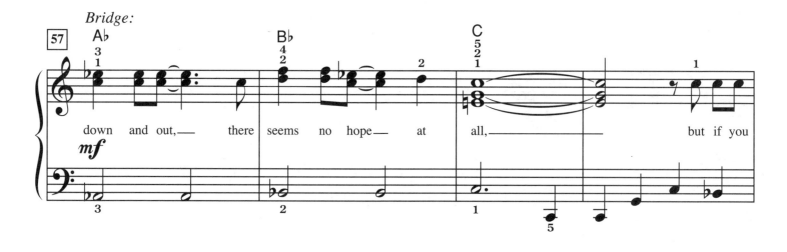

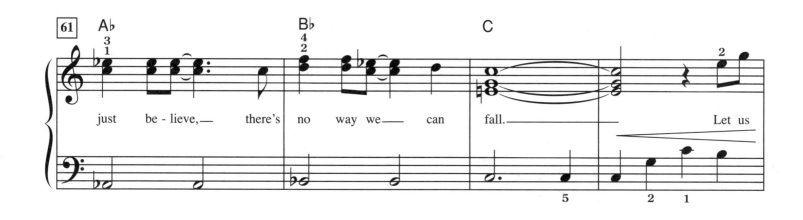

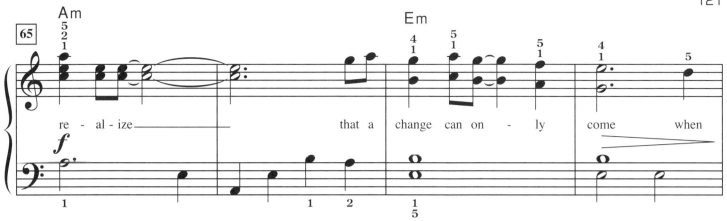

re - al - ize _____ that a change can on - ly come when

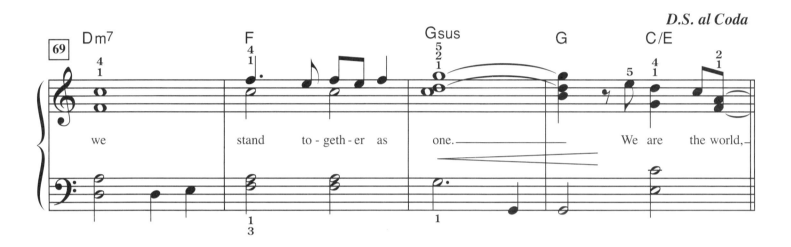

D.S. al Coda

we stand to - geth - er as one. _____ We are the world, _____

Coda

me. _____ It's _____ true, we'll make a bet - ter day, just you _____ and

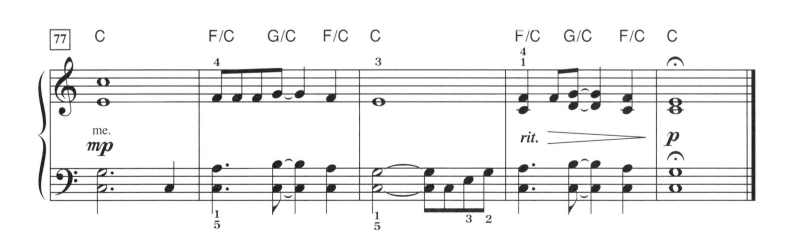

me.

THE WAY YOU MAKE ME FEEL

"The Way You Make Me Feel" was the third consecutive #1 single from Michael Jackson's ninth album *Bad* (1987). Jackson famously performed the single at the 1988 Grammy Awards, as well as at his 30th anniversary concert in 2001 at Madison Square Garden with Britney Spears. The success of the album was supported by Jackson's 16-month, 123-concert worldwide *The Bad Tour*, the most successful tour of the '80s which grossed over $125 million.

Written and Composed by Michael Jackson
Arranged by Dan Coates

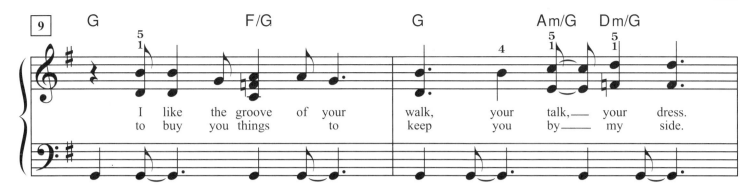

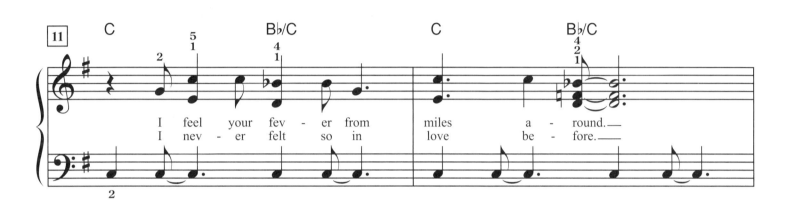

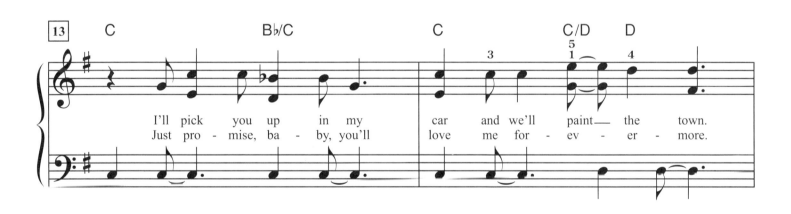

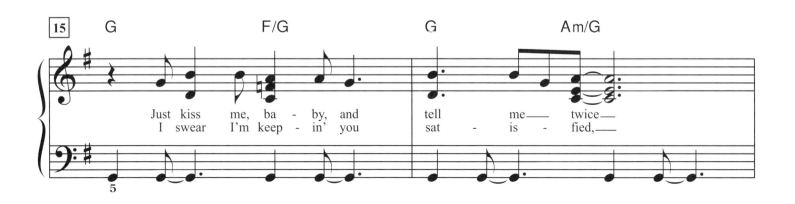

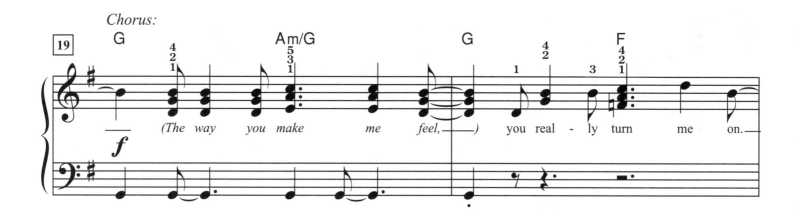

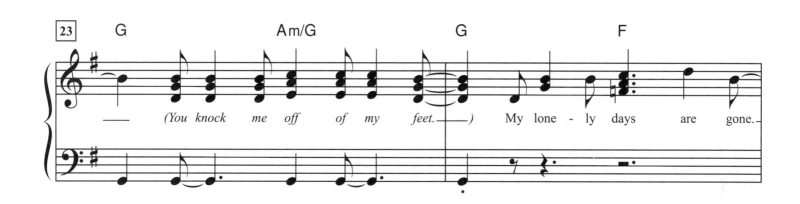

WHEN I SEE YOU SMILE

"When I See You Smile" is the biggest hit from the short-lived Los Angeles supergroup—a band consisting of members who have already achieved fame/musical respect—Bad English (1988–91). The power ballad is from their 1989 debut album *Bad English*. Their second album, *Backlash*, was released after the group had disbanded and was not as successful.

Words and Music by Diane Warren
Arranged by Dan Coates

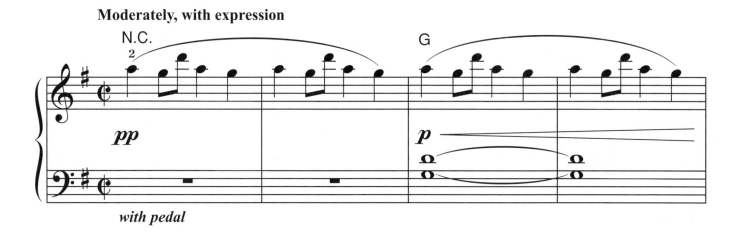

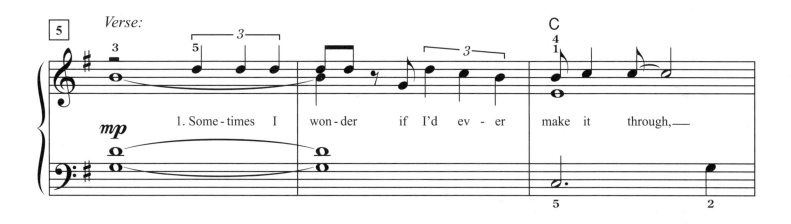

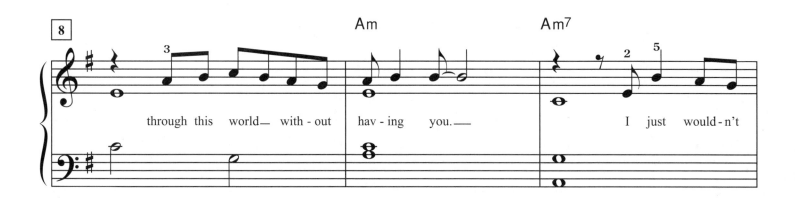

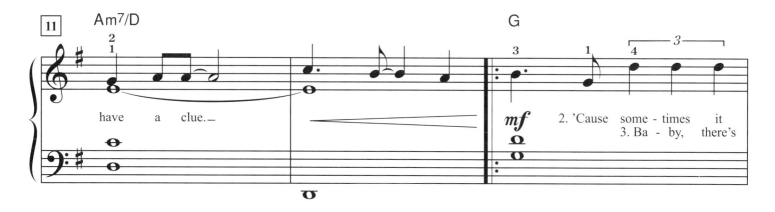

have a clue.—

mf 2. 'Cause some - times it
3. Ba - by, there's

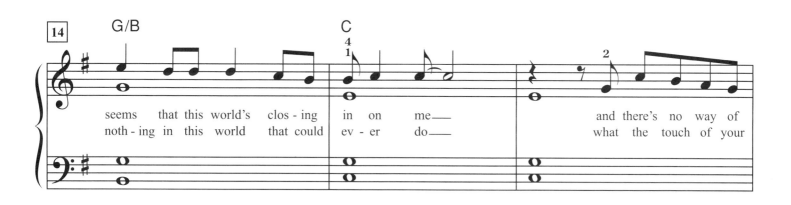

seems that this world's clos - ing in on me—— and there's no way of
noth - ing in this world that could ev - er do—— what the touch of your

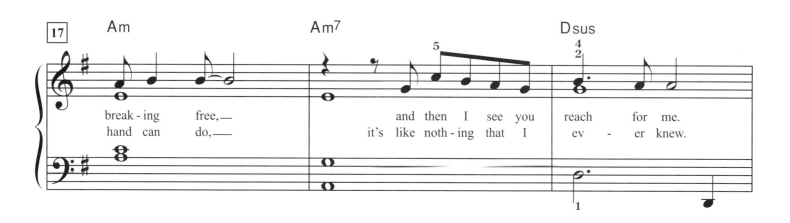

break - ing free,—— and then I see you reach for me.
hand can do,—— it's like noth - ing that I ev - er knew.

Bridge:

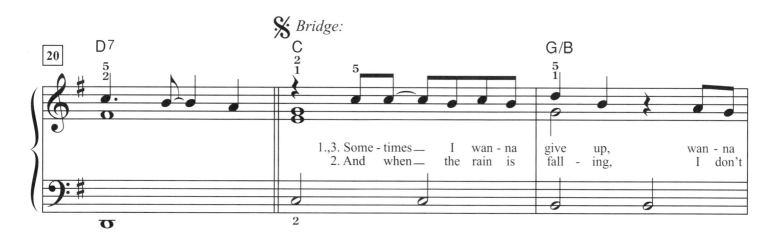

1.,3. Some - times—— I wan - na give up, wan - na
2. And when—— the rain is fall - ing, I don't

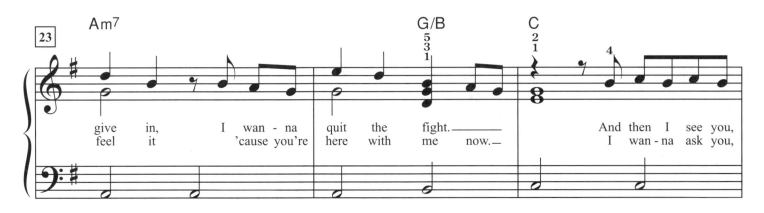

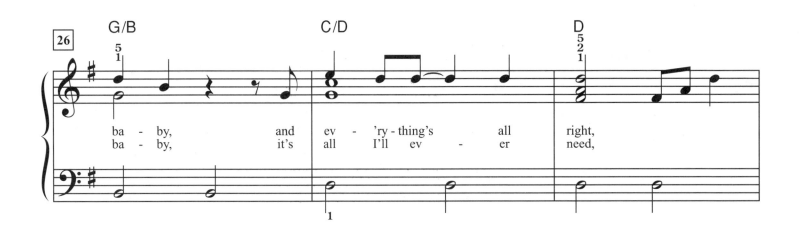

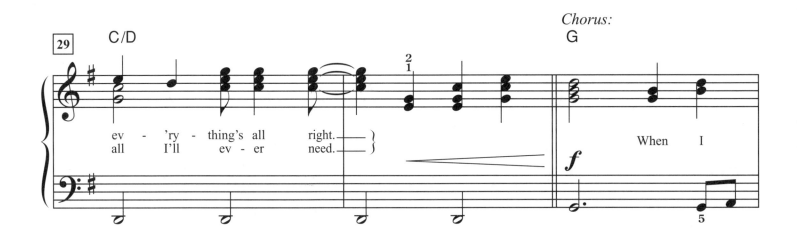

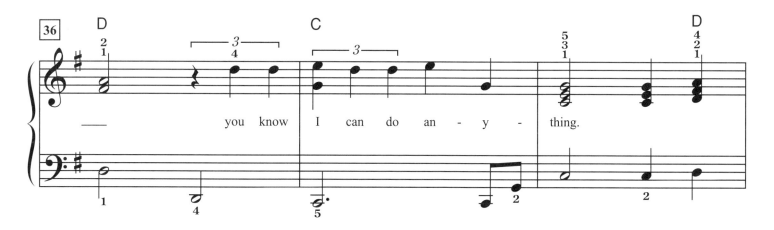

you know I can do an - y - thing.

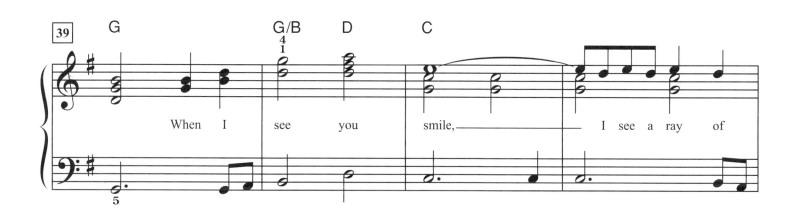

When I see you smile, I see a ray of

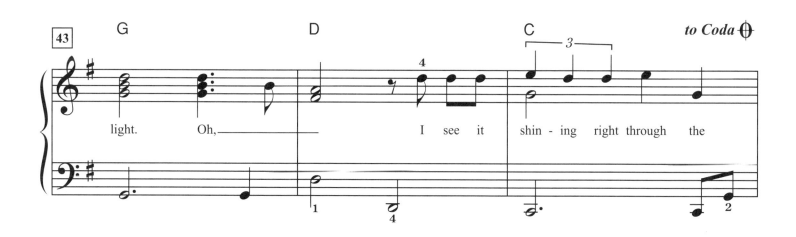

light. Oh, I see it shin - ing right through the

to Coda ⊕

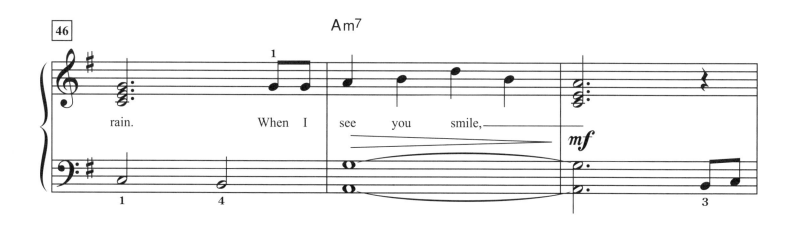

rain. When I see you smile,

_mf_

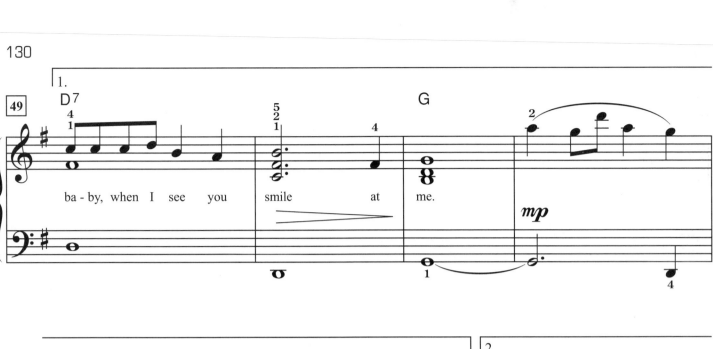

ba - by, when I see you smile at me.

mp

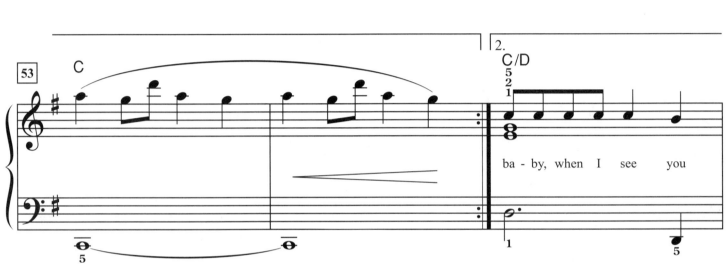

ba - by, when I see you

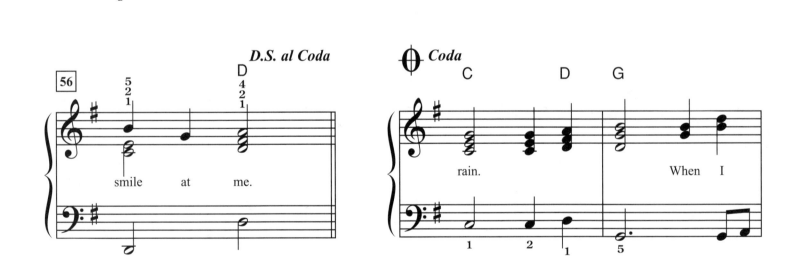

D.S. al Coda

smile at me.

Coda

rain.

When I

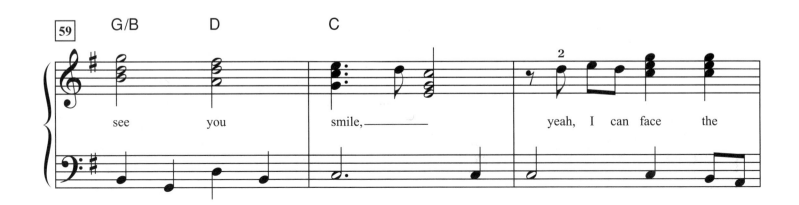

see you smile, yeah, I can face the

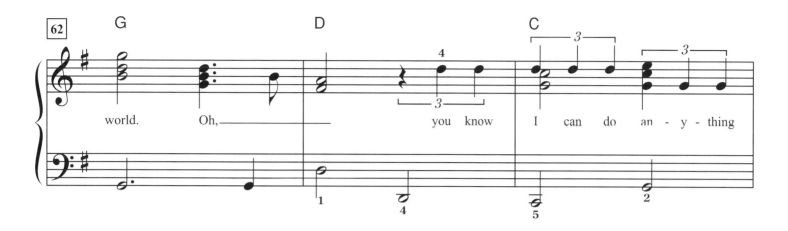

world. Oh, _____ you know I can do an - y - thing

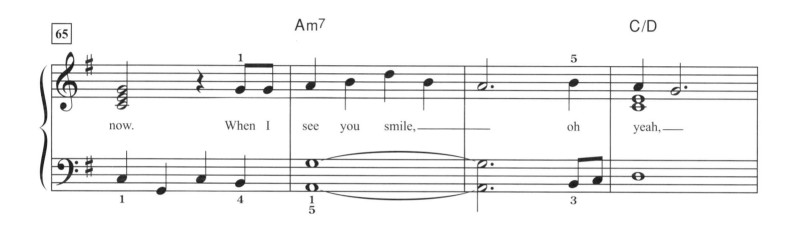

now. When I see you smile, _____ oh yeah, _____

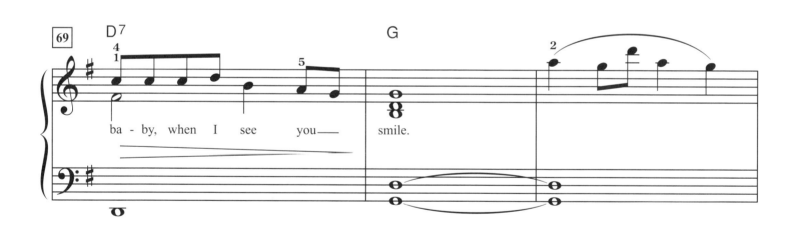

ba - by, when I see you _____ smile.

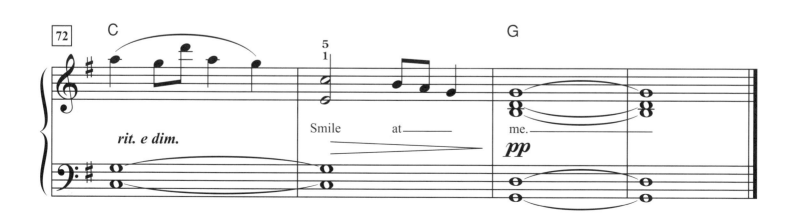

rit. e dim. Smile at _____ me. *pp*

WHO'S THAT GIRL

In contrast to the film of the same name, *Who's That Girl* (1987), the soundtrack, did remarkably well, selling over 6 million copies worldwide. In addition to starring in the movie, Madonna recorded the title song, which reached #1 in multiple countries. It was Madonna's 13th consecutive top 10 single. The *Who's That Girl* soundtrack also contained the hit "Causing a Commotion."

Words and Music by
Madonna Ciccone and Pat Leonard
Arranged by Dan Coates

133

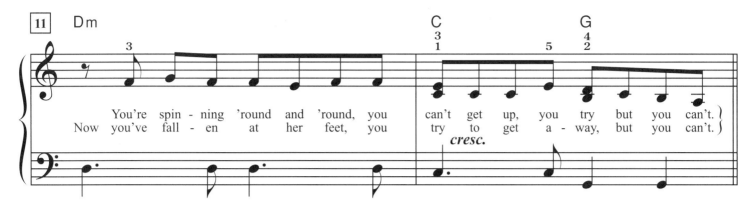

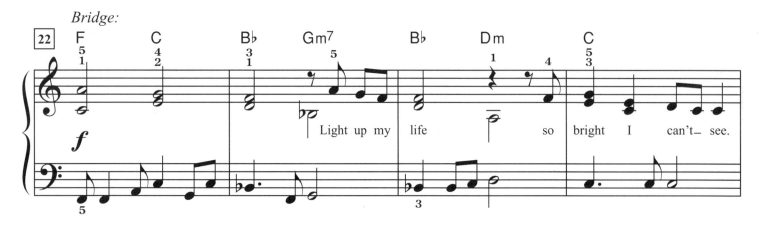

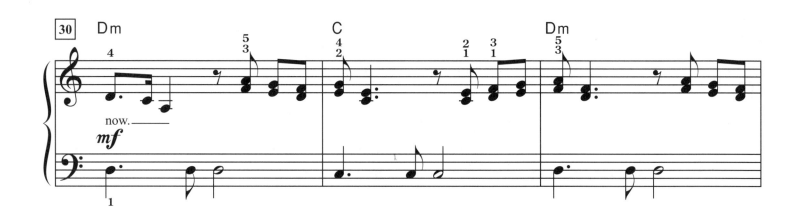

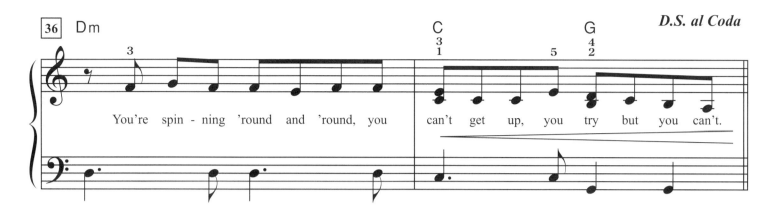

D.S. al Coda

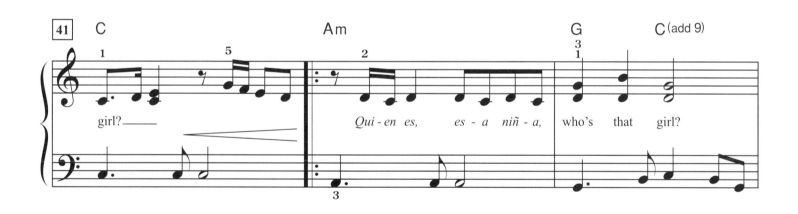

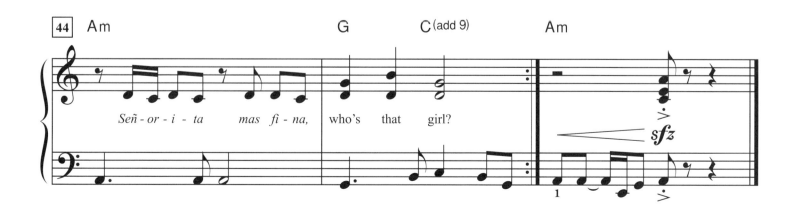

WIND BENEATH MY WINGS

"Wind Beneath My Wings" is known as Bette Midler's signature song. She recorded it in 1989 for the dramatic film *Beaches*, a movie in which she also starred. The single was a #1 hit and also won Record of the Year and Song of the Year at the 1990 Grammy Awards. A number of artists (Sheena Easton, Roger Whittaker, Gary Morris, Gladys Knight, and Lou Rawls) had recorded the song before Midler, yet none were as successful.

Words and Music by
Larry Henley and Jeff Silbar
Arranged by Dan Coates

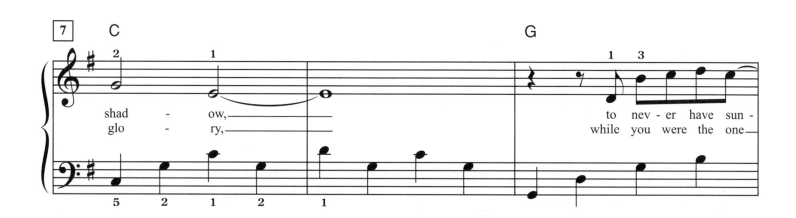

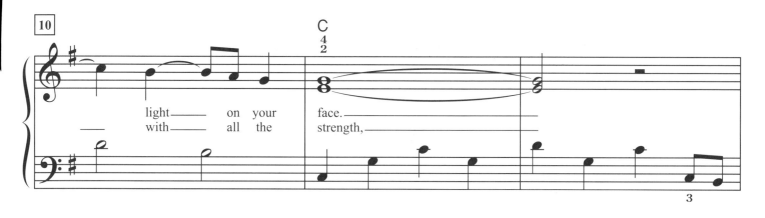

light———— on your face.————
with———— all the strength,————

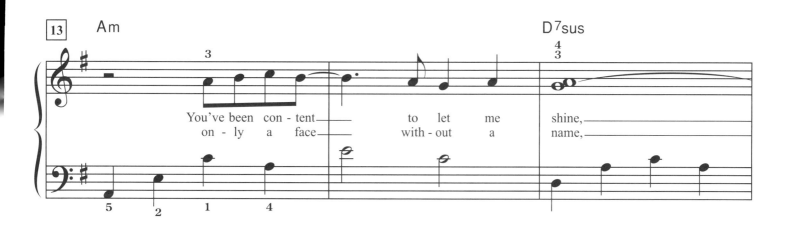

You've been con - tent———— to let me shine,————
on - ly a face———— with - out a name,————

you al - ways walked———— a step be -
I nev - er once———— heard you com -

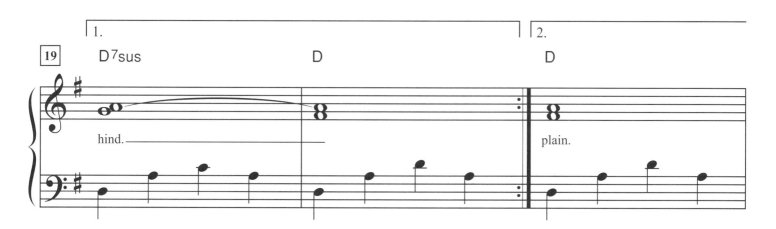

1.
hind. ————————

2.
plain.

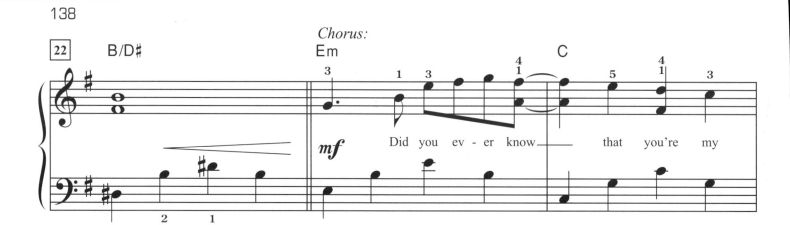

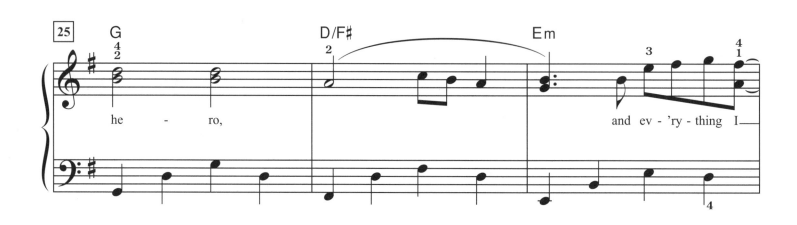

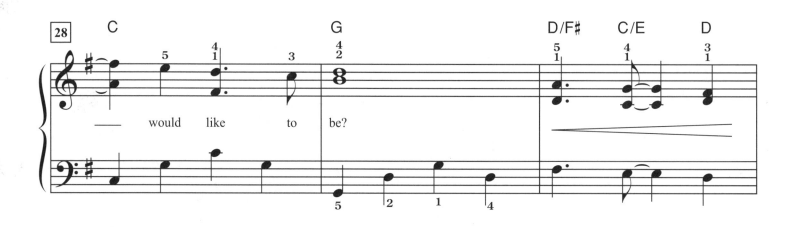

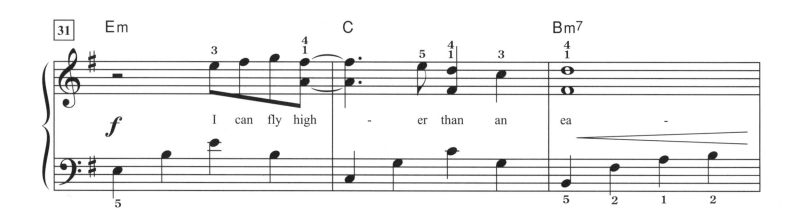

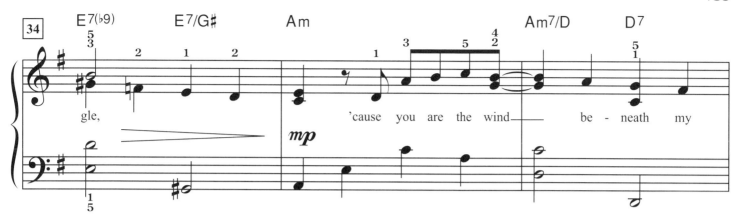

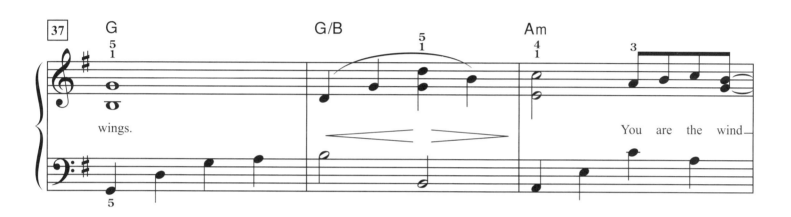

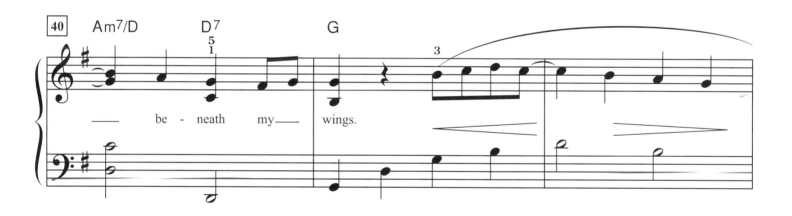

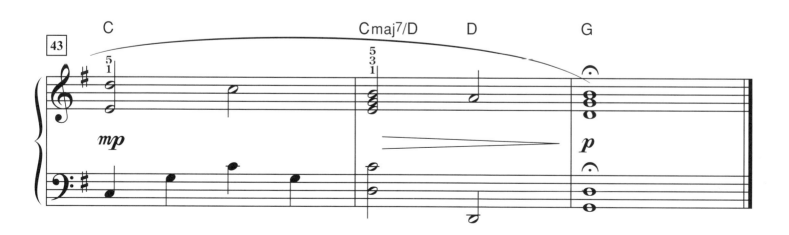

YOU ARE THE GIRL

"You Are the Girl" is the second single from the sixth and final studio album by The Cars, *Door to Door* (1987). The single made the top 20 in the charts, but The Cars would soon disband in February of 1988. Ric Ocasek, guitarist and lead singer, continued on to a solo career; David Robinson, drummer, retired from music; Benjamin Orr, bassist, passed away in 2000; Elliot Easton, lead/rhythm guitarist, and Greg Hawkes, keyboardist/saxophonist, formed The New Cars.

Words and Music by Ric Ocasek
Arranged by Dan Coates

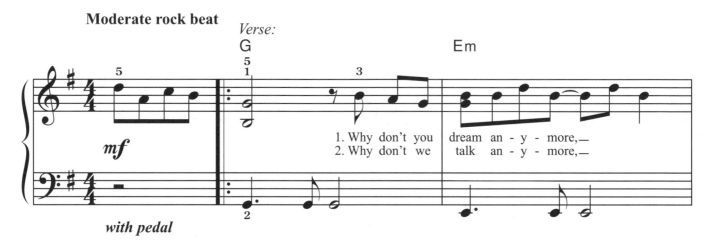

1. Why don't you dream an-y-more,—
2. Why don't we talk an-y-more,—

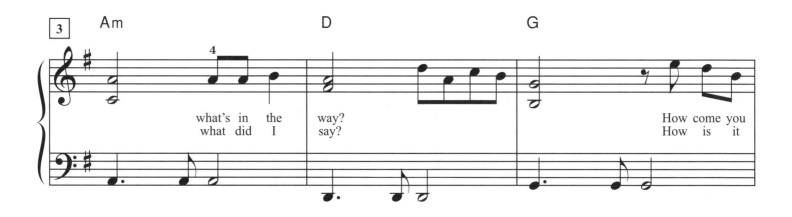

what's in the way? How come you
what did I say? How is it

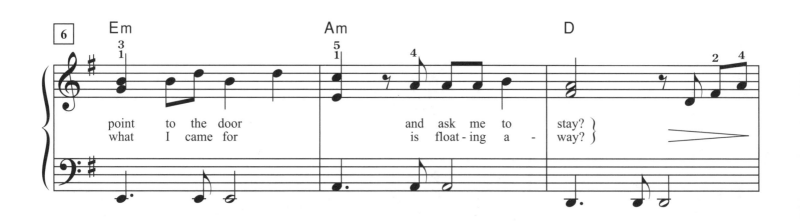

point to the door and ask me to stay?
what I came for is float-ing a - way?

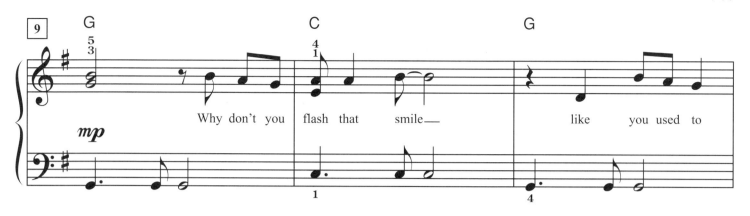

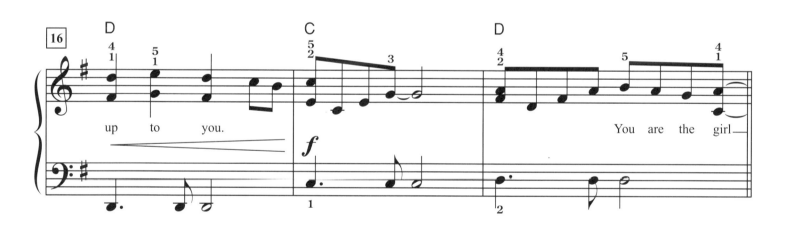

Chorus:

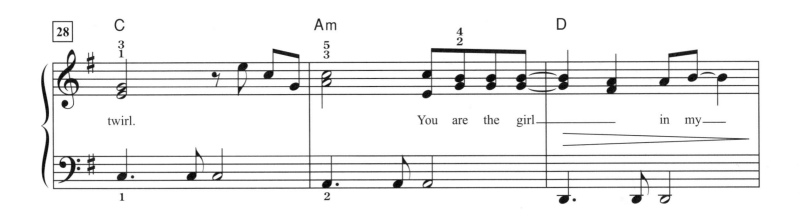

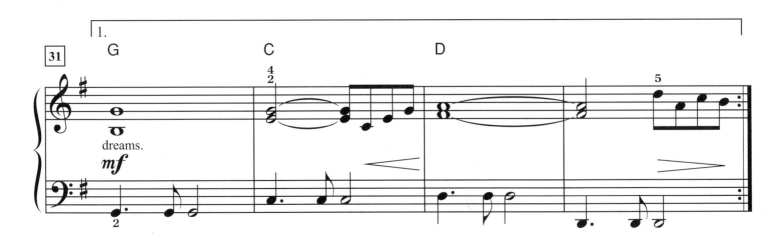

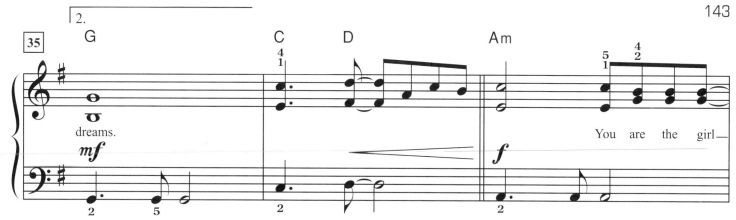

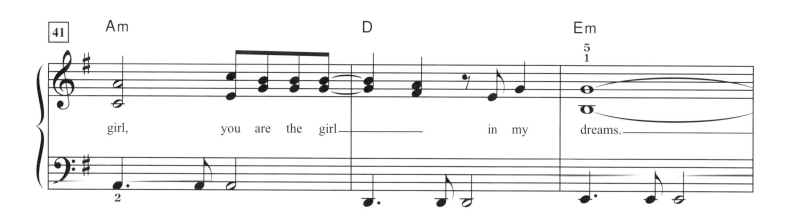

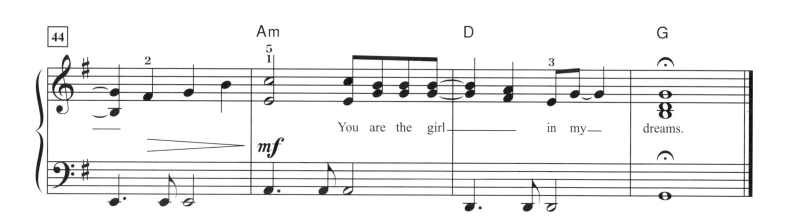